Growing-Up Years

The Princeton Center for Infancy is a self-supporting parent education group that researches and prepares books and pamphlets for parents and professionals. It was established by Frank Caplan, co-founder with his wife, Theresa Caplan, of Creative Playthings, Inc., and later president of the CBS Learning Center. From his experience there and his early training as one of the first male nursery-school teachers, he developed a deep interest in infancy and early childhood. For more than five years the Center's researchers have been building an infancy "data bank," collecting the most current research available on all child-rearing topics. Publications of the Princeton Center for Infancy include *The First Twelve Months of Life*, *The Parenting Advisor* and *Parents' Yellow Pages*. Frank and Theresa Caplan are authors of *The Power of Play* and *The Second Twelve Months of Life*.

A NOTE ON STYLE

The Princeton Center for Infancy is deeply committed to the principle that parents of both sexes assume responsibility for their child, as well as recognize the individuality of both male and female babies. We have uniformly used "parents" unless we are referring specifically to only the mother or father. For lack of a more appropriate universal pronoun, we have used "he" and "she" randomly when referring to babies.

YOUR CHILD'S RECORD-KEEPING BOOK

Growing-Up Years

Frank Caplan, General Editor

THE PRINCETON CENTER FOR INFANCY

Drawings and Calligraphy by Yaroslava

ANCHOR PRESS / DOUBLEDAY
Garden City, New York
1978

We are grateful for permission to use or adapt the following records:

from American College of Obstetricians, Gynecologists for Record #1
from American Academy of Pediatrics for Record #8
from American Association of Ophthalmology for Record #18
from Dr. M. Downs, Division of Otolaryngology, University of Colorado for Record #17
from American Dental Association for Record #26
from Dr. George Zimmer and Dr. Myrtle McGraw, formerly Briarcliff College for Records #28, 29, 96, 97, 98
from Dr. John Meier, Children's Village U.S.A. for Records #34, 35, 48, 95
from National Society for Prevention of Blindness for Record #37
from New York Chapter 3, American Academy of Pediatrics for Record #39
from Educators Publishing Company, "Developing Oral Language," by J. F. Murphy and C. A. O'Donnell for Record #52
from Project Headstart, U. S. Office of Child Development, HEW (no copyright claimed) for Records #24, 25, 41, 49, 51, 57, 64
from Dean's Office, University of Colorado Medical Center for Record #93
from Couple to Couple League for Record #97
from Ellen Peck and Delacorte Press, *The Joy of the Only Child* for Records #99, 100

Anchor Books Edition: 1978

Illustrations and cover design by Yaroslava Surmach Mills
Book design by Fran Gazze Nimeck

Library of Congress Catalog Card Number 77-15168
ISBN: 0-385-12411-2

Copyright © 1978 by the Princeton Center for Infancy and Early Childhood
All Rights Reserved
Printed in the United States of America
First Edition

Acknowledgements

Our search for an in-depth approach to records that would reflect parental attitudes, child health, language development, social behavior, etc. that parents could fill out, led us to several outstanding interdisciplinary professionals for advice, the review of our manuscript, and their contributions of adaptable test materials. We are deeply grateful for their help.

Robert J. Harmon, M.D., presently Special Fellow in Child Psychiatry, University of Colorado School of Medicine; formerly Research Associate, Social and Behavioral Sciences Branch, National Institute of Child Health and Human Development, and Clinical Instructor in Psychiatry and Behavioral Sciences, George Washington University. His precise review of the final manuscript and his supply of parent-child questionnaires have been invaluable.

Lewis Lipsitt, Ph.D., Professor of Psychology at Brown University and Director of the Child Study Center at St. Vincent de Paul Orphanage. His support of the idea of longitudinal studies led us to find ways of establishing two-way communication between early-childhood researchers and parents.

John H. Meier, Ph.D., former director, John F. Kennedy Child Development Center, and associate Professor of Pediatrics, Clinical Psychology and Education, University of Colorado Medical Center; also former director, U. S. Office of Child Development and chief of U. S. Children's Bureau, 1975-77. We adapted some of the fine behavior inventory records developed by him and his colleagues. His series of three books which make up the SOL Program (System for Open Learning) makes a major contribution to home and school curriculums for infancy and early-childhood education.

Virginia Shipman, Ph.D., Senior Research Psychologist and Chairman of the Early Learning and Social Research Group at the Educational Testing Service, Princeton, New Jersey. Her support of the use of parents as research collaborators led us to other records which have enriched this book.

Myrtle B. McGraw, Ph.D., psychologist and retired Director of the Baby Teaching Laboratory at Briarcliff College, Briarcliff Manor, New York. Her book, *Neuromuscular Maturation of the Human Infant*, is a classic in the field of infant motor development. We deeply appreciate her permission to use several of her observation guides.

We searched for some time for an artist who could add humor to the pages of this serious record-keeping book. It was well worth the effort. We found Yaroslava Surmach Mills, who did not only the illustrations, but the calligraphy and the cover design as well. Heartfelt thanks go to Loretta Barrett, Editorial Director of Anchor Press/Doubleday, for her enthusiastic response to our request to update the traditional baby book, and also to Angela Cox, Associate Editor.

The initial collecting, writing, and rewriting of this early-childhood record-keeping book fell into the concerned hands of Frank Caplan, Theresa Caplan, and Myra D. Hochman.

We extend special thanks to Dorothy J. Naylor, our steadfast typist and good friend.

PRINCETON CENTER FOR INFANCY Frank Caplan, General Editor
Theresa Caplan, Associate Editor, Myra D. Hochman, Formerly an Associate Editor

Contents

INTRODUCTION

PREGNANCY, BIRTH, AND THE NEWBORN

RECORD 1. Pregnancy, Labor, and Delivery 11
RECORD 2. Influences on Pregnancy 17
RECORD 3. Record of Birth 20
RECORD 4. Record of Adoption 21
RECORD 5. Photographic Record of Birth or Adoption 22
RECORD 6. Identification Marks on Newborn 23
RECORD 7. The First Day of Life—Hospital Chart 24
RECORD 8. Medical Examination at Birth 26
RECORD 9. Valuable Documents and Photos 30
RECORD 10. Feeding in Infancy 32
RECORD 11. Medical Check-ups 34
RECORD 12. Height and Growth Chart 36
RECORD 13. Weight and Growth Chart 38
RECORD 14. The Newborn's Reflexes 39

FIRST TWELVE MONTHS OF LIFE
MASTERING MOTOR AND SENSORY POWERS

RECORD 15. Growth and Development—First Twelve Months of Life 45
RECORD 16. Photographic Record 48
RECORD 17. Hearing Test—Birth to Eight Months 49
RECORD 18. Vision Record at Five Months 50
RECORD 19. Immunization Schedule 52
RECORD 20. Sleep Patterns in First Year 54
RECORD 21. Early Behavior Record—First to Third Months 56
RECORD 22. Visual-motor Skills 58
RECORD 23. Developing the Senses 60
RECORD 24. Seeing and Reaching Skills 62
RECORD 25. Patterns of Attachment 64
RECORD 26. Baby Teeth Formation 66

CONTENTS

SECOND TWELVE MONTHS OF LIFE—TODDLERS

RECORD 27. Growth and Development—Twelve to Twenty-four Months   71
RECORD 28. Crawling and Creeping   73
RECORD 29. Standing and Walking   76
RECORD 30. Sleep—Twelve to Twenty-four Months   78
RECORD 31. Home Hearing Test at Twelve and Twenty-four Months   80
RECORD 32. Fears and Dislikes   81

PLAY AND FANTASY—TWO TO FOUR YEARS

RECORD 33. Growth and Development—Two to Four Years   85
RECORD 34. First Nursery School/Child-care Center   88
RECORD 35. Preschool and Kindergarten Interests and Activities   91
RECORD 36. Periodic Preschool Physical Exams—Two to Five Years   94
RECORD 37. Eye Test—The "E" Game   96
RECORD 38. Visiting the Ophthalmologist   98

THE LEARNING CHILD—FIRST THREE YEARS

RECORD 39. Developmental Landmarks in First Three Years   103
RECORD 40. Language Acquisition During First Three Years   105
RECORD 41. Communication Skills   107
RECORD 42. The Playing Child—Birth to Three Years   109
RECORD 43. Motor Accomplishments   112
RECORD 44. Parents' Role in Learning   114

THE CREATIVE YEARS—FOUR TO SIX

RECORD 45. Growth and Development—Four to Six Years   119
RECORD 46. The Playing Child—Four to Eight Years   123
RECORD 47. Social Skills at the Preschool Level   126
RECORD 48. Preschool Personality Development   129
RECORD 49. Preschool Health Examination—Bones and Posture Record   132
RECORD 50. Preschool or School Dental Health Record   134

CONTENTS

RECORD 51. Care of Permanent Teeth *136*
RECORD 52. Self-image *138*
RECORD 53. Attending Kindergarten *141*
RECORD 54. Home Behavior Checklist—Ages Four to Six *142*
RECORD 55. School Behavior Checklist—Ages Four to Six *144*
RECORD 56. First-grade Achievements *146*
RECORD 57. Teacher's Health Observations *147*

MILESTONES AND MEMORIES

RECORD 58. Photo Gallery *151*
RECORD 59. "First Times" in Your Early Life *154*
RECORD 60. Early Art-Efforts *156*
RECORD 61. Favorite Books *161*

THE ACADEMIC YEARS—SIX TO NINE

RECORD 62. Growth and Development—Six to Nine Years *165*
RECORD 63. School Tests and Records *168*
RECORD 64. The Emerging Personality *171*
RECORD 65. A Record About Me *172*

ADOLESCENCE—NINE TO SIXTEEN YEARS

RECORD 66. Growth and Development—Nine to Twelve Years *179*
RECORD 67. Growth and Development—Twelve to Sixteen Years *182*
RECORD 68. A "Self" Inventory—Nine to Twelve Years *186*

THE FAMILY

RECORD 69. Father and His Predecessors *191*
RECORD 70. Mother and Her Predecessors *196*
RECORD 71. Fathering *201*
RECORD 72. The Consistent Caretaker *203*

CONTENTS

RECORD 73. Brothers and Sisters (Sibling Rivalry) *206*
RECORD 74. Parents' Attitudes Toward Child Rearing *207*
RECORD 75. Parents' Attitudes Toward Racial and Cultural Differences *212*
RECORD 76. Parents' Attitudes Toward Their Sex Roles *214*
RECORD 77. Spiritual and Religious Experiences *217*
RECORD 78. Christmas or Hanukkah and Other Celebrations *218*
RECORD 79 Record of Family Residences *220*
RECORD 80 Family Pets *221*
RECORD 81. Vacations with the Family *222*
RECORD 82. Vacations Away from the Family (with relatives, friends, at camp) *223*
RECORD 83. Parents' Reminiscences *224*

MEDICAL AND LEGAL RECORDS

RECORD 84. Family Photo Tree *230*
RECORD 85. Family Medical Chart *232*
RECORD 86. Allergy History *234*
RECORD 87. Illnesses and X-rays *235*
RECORD 88. Hospital Admissions *237*
RECORD 89. Child's Accidents and Surgery *238*
RECORD 90. Accidents, Negligence, Court Claims *239*
RECORD 91. Citizenship Record *241*
RECORD 92. Wills, Inheritances, and Legal Guardianship *243*

APPENDIX

RECORD 93. Denver Developmental Screening Test *249*
RECORD 94. Breast-feeding Survey *254*
RECORD 95. Evaluation of Your Child's Learning and Development *256*
RECORD 96. Guide for Observing Motor Development *258*
RECORD 97. Observing Eye-hand Co-ordination *262*
RECORD 98. Observation Guide on Standing *264*
RECORD 99. Questionnaire for Only Children *266*
RECORD 100. Questionnaire for Parents of Only Children *269*

GLOSSARY *272*

In the pages that follow, we have recorded all the important facts and events in your early life that contributed to your growth and development.

Some of the child-rearing specialists during your babyhood, especially members of the medical profession, put great stock in the genetic weaknesses and strengths that you inherited from your forebears. Others—psychologists, educators, psychoanalysts—claim that environmental factors (parents, people, objects, encounters) are the main determinants of a child's responses and behavior.

Since child-rearing is not an exact science, we have read the available literature in this challenging field and have developed a "sixth sense" to help us make full use of the care-giving advice that will best suit your special character and needs.

We have tried in this record-keeping book to give you all the salient facts about yourself that you should find useful and interesting. Many of them may explain or shed light on situations or developments that may arise in your adult life.

If the records seem subjective (and this may well be the case) it is because, as your parents, we gave fully of our love, concern, and care. We enriched your environment and experiences as best we could. We pulled you out of childhood illnesses and accidents and encouraged your progress every step of the way. We cheered your attempts and accomplishments by our love, encouragement, and approval. Hopefully our guidance during your childhood will enable you to make intelligent, satisfying life decisions throughout your adulthood.

The lined introductory pages throughout this book allow a parent to record a very personal statement about the memories, joys, and sorrows during a particular period of time in the child's life.

We hope you enjoy this uniquely personal book. It should help you understand what makes you "tick."

Compiled by _____
_____
_____

Introduction

Many baby books are fine momentos for sharing with relatives and friends the excitement of the birth and early development of your child. Too often, however, they lack the depth, content, and essential details that can help you cope with the varied physical, psychological, and other situations all parents continuously face while rearing their children.

Why Keep Records?

The Princeton Center for Infancy has created a very special record-keeping book that will not only provide your grown child with a complete infancy-through-adolescence health and growth record, but will contribute to his or her self-awareness and self-esteem. By sharing your mutual achievements, delights, disappointments, and frustrations, you will be helping your offspring gain perspective about the present in relation to the past (and the future). This insight enables a child to comprehend the complex problems of parenthood as well as his own identity. Every experience your child has had throughout the early years with the world of people and things and all the developmental changes he has undergone will combine meaningfully to contribute to this invaluable "life-script." Your grown child will appreciate having data he would be unable otherwise to recall. In turn, filling out this record-keeping book will provide you with practical parenting techniques for understanding the "ages and stages" of childhood and help make you a better parent in the process.

Most parents keep some records, because these can help them recall (for medical and/or educational purposes) those diseases, illnesses, accidents, inoculations, etc. that are important for professional diagnosis as new conditions arise. Doctors and hospitals usually record every health event, but when parents move from place to place and change doctors, or when doctors die, or move their practices, records are lost to the parents. Children may be treated in many hospitals and have tests performed in various laboratories so that it becomes almost impossible to remember where they all are. Today's doctors believe that to protect one's health, it is essential to keep accurate records of drugs and medications taken, and exposure to radiation (X-rays, etc.) that medical researchers find injurious.

However, there are many requirements for a creative, responsible, happy life (including one's emotional, social, and learning adjustments throughout the early years) that significantly influence adjustment in adulthood. Therefore, we are devoting many pages for recording such non-health areas as the onset of language, fears, or parent-child relationships, etc. that may shed light upon your child's adult behavior. The data you collect about physical and mental changes will prove indispensable.

When your daughter is an adult and plans to have a baby, she will need her early history to share with her obstetrician. Should your son approach his middle years and be faced with the onset of some illness, whether it be heart failure, cancer, or a nervous breakdown, he would wish he had medical records of his mother's pregnancy, his father's physical and mental conditions, or his brother's or sister's feelings of depression. When your child enters school and joins in

INTRODUCTION

athletic events, he will have to answer questions that only this book can reveal. When your grown child applies for a sensitive government or other position and needs to list the family's multiple residences on the application, you will be thanked for taking the time to keep this record-keeping book up to date.

How To Keep Records

Whether aware of it or not, all parents keep informal records of their children—as they discuss tiny growth "breakthroughs" with relatives, take pictures to permanently preserve special moments and occasions, and jot down the poetic phrases, original lyrics, or creative discoveries their children express verbally. This record-keeping book will systematically assist in this procedure and provide a permanent "data bank."

Familiarize yourself with the subjects treated, some of which might not have crossed your mind heretofore. You will find that the subjects are arranged chronologically whenever possible (so that the prenatal period is followed by birth, for example). There are also general categories for records covering long spans of time (such as *Milestones and Memories*). Each record is introduced by an "Editor's Note" to give you information about the particular record and an explanation of the procedure involved. Space requirements necessitate abbreviated introductions. We at The Princeton Center for Infancy recommend that you turn to other Princeton Center for Infancy child-rearing books, such as *The Power of Play, The Parenting Advisor, Parents' Yellow Pages* (Anchor Press/Doubleday), and *The First Twelve Months of Life* and *The Second Twelve Months of Life* (Grosset & Dunlap), for fuller explanations of these issues.

As you periodically observe and record your baby's emerging abilities, you will increase your own sensitivity and appreciation of her progress and your ability to enrich your child's environment and thus maximize her potential. "Making a match" between the child and her physical, psychological, and other needs is a professional art, the single most important "sixth sense" for parents to develop.

Above all, enjoy recording the growth and development of your child. Ignore timetables and do not worry about your child's progress. For instance, some children skip stages entirely; others regress when their status is challenged by a newborn in the family or illness. "Growth," says Dr. Myrtle B. McGraw, "is not a straight onward and upward one of development. It is a jagged process of spurts and regressions. Older is not necessarily more advanced. Behavior need not occur at a specific month."

Researcher's Records

You will note that, in the Appendix and throughout the book, is a series of forms called "Researcher's Records" that can be of particular interest to infancy researchers. These records provide vital data that can have bearing on our country's decisions on educational, medical, and mental health plans and priorities. Most researchers dream of the day when the federal government will provide sufficient funds to trace medical, learning, and emotional behaviors from infancy through adulthood. Such studies are called "longitudinal studies." Practically none exist at present because they are extremely costly.

As a result of accurate observations and record-keeping by doctors, infant researchers, and

INTRODUCTION

other disciplines, medical science has come a long way in understanding childhood health, development, and behavior. Dr. Jean Piaget, the Swiss psychologist, has developed numerous theories of education by observing and recording the growth and learning patterns of his own three children week by week. Such early data are vital to filling in the gaps in professional knowledge about child health, learning, and personal and social development.

Who better than parents can conduct "longitudinal" studies? No one! Therefore, we have included behavior inventories, observation guides, and other studies that will help your child know more of her early life and at the same time add to the data sought by researchers. In this way you will be helping us amass a sampling of important data on children's growth and development that would be almost impossible for an infant researcher to accumulate in a laboratory setting. If possible, please Xerox or otherwise duplicate the completed pages in this section and return them to The Princeton Center for Infancy, 306 Alexander Street, Princeton, New Jersey 08540. We will forward these filled-out Researcher's Records to professionals studying these areas for their analysis and use. We will respect your confidentiality if you do not care to reveal the name of your child.

Professional Records and Medical Information

"Professional Records" (some are located in the Appendix) are to be filled out by professionals: doctors, dentists, ophthalmologists, nursery school and kindergarten teachers, etc. Many of these require careful, ongoing professional observation and take time to fill out. You will have to enlist the professional's assistance (nurse or others) to collect such information for you.

Doctors, dentists, and other professionals are very busy people. In order to make their job a little easier, we suggest that you photocopy at your local public library (cost is about $.05 to $.10 per page) those pages that cover medical data. At your next office visit, just leave a copy with your doctor's nurse and pick it up at your convenience when it has been completed. Then you can staple the filled-out copy to the matched page contained herein or fill in the blank form with information received.

[Please note that Xerox copy centers or draftsmen supply houses use duplicating machines (Eastman Kodak and others) that copy two pages of a book simultaneously by reducing the original book copy by one third. This allows you to staple the reduced copy to the page number listed at the top. Reducing cost is slightly higher: $.15 to $.20.]

Thanks to new Health, Education, and Welfare Department regulations for the Family Rights and Privacy Act of 1974, parents now have access to what was previously intended only for the eyes of teachers and school administrators. Now schools and other institutions are required to make available any tests or progress reports to parents who request them. Parents and students (if over eighteen) may view the student's academic record as long as the school receives funds from the U.S. Commissioner of Education.

Taking advantage of this new ruling is an important step for parents who wish to retain influence over their children's educational growth. If you find any unfair or false information in your child's file, you have a right to ask that it be changed or removed altogether. If the school refuses, you may obtain a hearing with a school officer not involved in the preparation of the original report. Even if the school should decide to keep the information on record, you may write a rebuttal which is retained in the file attached to the offending document.

INTRODUCTION

How To Use This Record-keeping Book

Once your child is old enough (of high school or college age), if you wish, you may present these records to him. When your adult child becomes a parent, he may want to share with his own child what went into the "making of an adult."

Throughout this record-keeping book (under "Editor's Notes") and in all our publications, the Princeton Center for Infancy point of view is expressed both in the text and the themes we choose to emphasize. Child-rearing is not yet a precise science (or art), and until more research is forthcoming, your (or our) intuition will have to prevail.

There are records devoted to parent attitudes toward child-rearing, sex, and morals that some parents may consider too personal to share with children. Some records attempt to inventory family financial and legal matters. Certainly you are not obliged to fill out every page, but what you do record will be much more than what previous generations wrote down. Any pages that you decide you do not wish to share with your grown-up offspring can be torn out along the vertical side (1 inch from the binding) so as to keep the book intact.

Some records were inserted to give parents some insight into the "ages and stages" of growth. Even if these may not be meaningful to your adult son or daughter (although they should), you will learn so much from filling them out that we deliberately included them. One or two records attempt to reflect your child's opinions; these will require your child's co-operation.

Other Kinds of Records

Of course, there are other kinds of childhood records that parents should keep. Below are some of them:

Voice recordings on cassettes: If you have or can locate a cassette tape recorder, you will want to make a recording of your child's voice—her babbling sounds, beginning words, singing and reciting nursery rhymes, etc.—as she grows into adolescence. Remember to include parent-child and grandparent-child discussions, peer group conversations, and so on. Should you desire to edit and retain the best of this oral history, seek the help of a sound laboratory technician who with your help can cut and splice the best parts into a half-hour- to hour-long cassette.

Photography: A photographic record of your child will be appreciated by all concerned and most especially by your grandchildren when they appear on the scene. If you find all this too complicated, you can take advantage of "booth photography" located in various public places, where you can get four pictures at different angles and moods.

To reproduce, enlarge, or reduce a photo: Paste a piece of transparent paper (Scotch-tape it on back) over the positive picture or print. Circle or square only the area of the picture to be blown up or reduced. You may want just the head of a child or adult or a section of a group picture. This technique allows a photographer to blow up, block out, or reduce a picture to the desired size. Specify on the transparent overlay the size you want in inches (for example, 2¼" x 2¼") to be blown up or reduced. Remember to send along the negative. The negative and positive will be returned to you by the film-processing house you use.

Creative enterprises: Keep a large scrapbook of your child's early scribbles, drawings, paintings, collages, and so on.

INTRODUCTION

Anecdotes: Keep a running diary of your child's poetry, songs, and stories.

Genealogy—Searching Out Family Origins

At a time when family life seems increasingly threatened and Americans become more and more rootless, many people are establishing ties with their past by searching out and recording their genealogical origins. You can give your child a sense of where he comes from and a feeling of family belonging by beginning a family tree of your own.

Genealogy can be as simple or as involved a hobby as you care to make it. Here are some suggestions for newcomers to the "tree-climbing" sport. The first step is to either purchase or make a set of "pedigree and family group sheets." These indicate where names, dates, and other vital information should be placed on the family tree. They can be obtained through office-supply stores and some libraries.

The search begins with family members and friends who can remember information that you do not. While interviewing older relatives, ask them for their family records. Bibles often contain valuable genealogical information.

After the family memories have been exhausted, there are many other sources of information which you can search as time and inclination allow. The public library is a good place to look. Newspapers, telephone books, census records, and sometimes even a genealogy collection can provide a wealth of information. For instance, obituary notices in old newspapers may contain other valuable facts about your ancestors besides the date of death. County records offices will be able to give you civil records, such as marriage licenses, death certificates, and wills. Churches and temples keep records of births, baptisms, bar mitzvahs, and marriages. Gravestones in your local cemetery may also give you clues to your past.

If you really become involved with the hunt, ask at your public library for listings of local and national genealogical societies as well as names of genealogical magazines in which you can place ads for family information and pick up family hunting hints.

Enjoy the search and remember that as your family tree grows so does your child's sense of belonging to a definite past.

Storing and Safeguarding Family Records

It is important for every family to know what records are necessary to save and whether they should be kept at home or in a safety deposit box at the bank. Some suggestions follow, but a good rule of thumb would seem to be: If it cannot be replaced or would be difficult to do so, keep it in a safety deposit box. If not, file it at home.

Some important documents that should be kept in a safety deposit box include: birth and marriage certificates, divorce decrees, adoption papers, citizenship and military service records, stock certificates and bonds, savings certificates and passbooks, and insurance policies.

Education and employment records, income tax returns, canceled checks, social security cards and passports can be kept in a file at home.

It should be pointed out that original signed wills should be filed with one's lawyer, with carbon copies kept both at home and in a safety deposit box.

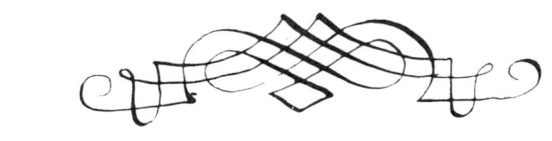

PREGNANCY, BIRTH, AND THE NEWBORN

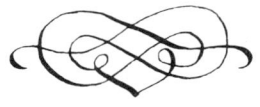

RECORD 1   Recorder _____   11

Pregnancy, Labor, and Delivery
(TO BE FILLED OUT BY OBSTETRICIAN OR HOSPITAL DOCTOR)
(A Professional Record)

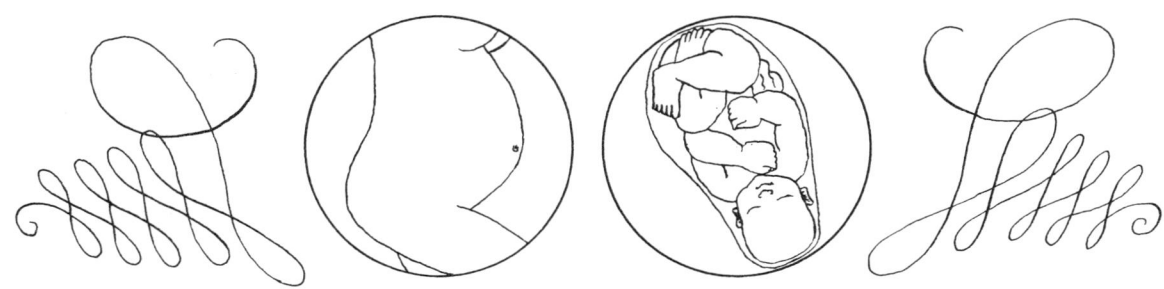

EDITOR'S NOTE *Many prenatal influences affect the growing baby. This particular record is of importance to both mother and baby and might be useful to the pediatrician. If you cannot remember some information, ask your obstetrician or clinic doctor for help. If your doctor is too busy, make a Xerox copy and leave it with him or her to fill out at leisure.*

Menstrual History

Onset _____   Frequency _____   Duration _____
Problems _____
Date of Last Menstrual Period _____   Expected Date of Delivery _____

Birth Control Prior to Pregnancy

Type _____   How Long Used _____
When Stopped _____   Problems _____

Medication during pregnancy	Dates	Amount	What stage of pregnancy
vitamins	_____	_____	_____
iron	_____	_____	_____
aspirin	_____	_____	_____
antihistamines	_____	_____	_____
others	_____	_____	_____
chest X-ray	_____	_____	_____
other X-rays	_____	_____	_____

RECORD 1 (CONTINUED)

Problems and illnesses during pregnancy   *Occurred when*   *How treated*

vomiting (morning sickness)   _____   _____

excessive weight gain _____ lbs. _____ oz.   _____   _____

excessive weight loss _____ lbs. _____ oz.   _____   _____

headaches   _____   _____

dizziness   _____   _____

spotting (bleeding)   _____   _____

swelling (puffiness)   _____   _____

others   _____   _____

Special diet _____

_____

Lab-tests during pregnancy

"Pap" smear test _____

Others _____

_____

Blood grouping and types _____

Mother _____ blood type _____ Rh factor _____ blood count

Father _____ blood type _____ Rh factor _____ blood count

Blood tests for syphilis _____ Other _____

| *Length of pregnancy* (circle) | 28 wks. or less | 29 to 32 wks. | 33 to 36 wks. | full term (40 wks.) | 1 to 2 wks. past mature | 3 wks. or more past mature |

Past Medical History

Childhood Illnesses _____

Hospitalization _____

Serious Illnesses _____ Chronic Medical Problems _____

_____

Remarks _____

Family History (congenital defects, current illnesses)

Parents _____

Current Illnesses _____

Mother's OB history _____ Sister's OB history _____

RECORD 1 (CONTINUED)

Previous Pregnancies

Del. Date	Character of Pregnancy	Type of Labor	Length of Labor	Weight Gain	Baby Weight	Medication Episiotomy	Complications	Sex

Were babies breastfed? _____

Miscarriages and Abortions

Date	Cause	Complications

Did you take diethyl stilbesterol (DES)? Check _____ Yes _____ No

Aids used during difficult prenatal periods (products, books, interpersonal) _____
_____
_____
_____

NATURE OF LABOR AND DELIVERY

Reason for seeking home birth or hospital birth _____

Date _____ Describe onset of labor _____

Labor—duration _____ less than 3 hours _____ 3 to 23 hours _____ 29 hours or more

spontaneous onset _____ induced _____

Membranes ruptured _____ date _____ time _____ FHT _____

Position of baby _____ vertex _____ breech _____ transverse

Medication during labor _____
_____

Method of delivery:

Vaginal _____ Forceps _____ Caesarean section _____

Type of anesthesia used (if any) _____

Total time on delivery table _____

RECORD 1 (CONTINUED) 14

Note complications (if any) during labor and birth _____

_____

If mother is Rh Negative, note if any of the following were done:

Antibody test _____ When _____ normal _____ abnormal _____

Anti-Rh factor _____ When _____ normal _____ abnormal _____

Amniocentesis _____ When _____ normal _____ abnormal _____

Rho Gam _____ When _____ normal _____ abnormal _____

Mother—medications and drugs

Prescribed for hospital use _____

_____

_____

Prescribed for use at home _____

_____

Mother—problems

bleeding _____ breasts _____

fever _____ hemorrhoids _____

cord clamped—minutes after birth _____ placenta _____

other _____

Describe delivery room environment and mother's and father's emotional state (for example did hospital practice Leboyer delivery method of "birth without violence": soft lights, muted sounds and voices, warm bath for newborn, massage, etc.?) _____

_____

_____

_____

_____

Unusual events at birth _____

_____

_____

_____

_____

Attending Doctor's Name _____ Address _____

City, State, Zip _____ Telephone _____

Attending Midwife's Name _____ Address _____

City, State, Zip _____ Telephone _____

RECORD 1 (CONTINUED) 15

Delivery Follow-up

Appointment with Dr. _____

Time _____ Date _____ Address _____

Problems, if any:
_____
_____
_____

Treatment or discussion _____
_____
_____
_____

Appointment with Dr. _____

Time _____ Date _____ Address _____

Problems, if any:
_____
_____
_____

Treatment or discussion _____
_____
_____
_____

Appointment with Dr. _____

Time _____ Date _____ Address _____

Problems, if any:
_____
_____
_____

Treatment or discussion _____
_____
_____
_____

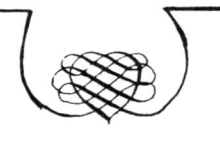

Photos
during
pregnancy

RECORD 2   Recorder _____   17

Influences on Pregnancy*
(A Researcher's Record)

EDITOR'S NOTE *Our grandmothers urged pregnant women to attend Bach concerts and visit art museums in order to produce "cultured" babies and to maintain "serene" and "placid" emotional states if they desired similarly disposed babies. Current research partially agrees with Grandma! It has been discovered that many positive and negative environmental aspects of prenatal life influence the future physical and psychological health of a baby. Now is the time to exercise extreme caution. Try to avoid all drugs during early pregnancy unless specifically prescribed by your obstetrician (e.g., vitamins, iron, Benetin for nausea, etc.). Avoid emotional stress if and when possible.*

Mother's age at conception _____

External influences on fetus

First sign of life: Date _____ Describe _____
_____

When you first felt your baby move _____

Active reaction to sound: Date _____ Describe _____
_____

Active reaction to light: Date _____ Describe _____
_____

Most active time of day _____ Describe _____
_____

*Fill out this record during your pregnancy.

RECORD 2 (CONTINUED)

Environmental factors

Chemical Agents: included as drugs are aspirin, antihistamines, tranquilizers, laxatives, nasal decongestants, and antivomit agents.

Drug Taken	Month of Pregnancy	Reason for Use
_____	_____	_____
_____	_____	_____
_____	_____	_____
_____	_____	_____

Tobacco (If you are a smoker, try to stop!):
nonsmoker _____ moderate _____ light smoker _____ heavy _____
comments _____

Cultural Influences (practicing piano daily, etc.):
_____
_____
_____
_____

Emotional factors

Stress events (separation, divorce, death in family, accident, job loss, etc.):
Describe situation _____
_____
_____
_____
_____
_____

Do you like _____ or dislike _____ being pregnant?
Is this a good time in your life to be pregnant? _____
Explain _____
_____
_____

Do you have a job outside the home? Yes _____ No _____ Part-time _____ Full-time _____
Nature of employment _____
_____

RECORD 2 (CONTINUED)

_____
_____

Do you rest daily? _____
Do you have help at home? _____
How much? _____

Fetal Behavior Due to Mother's Activities

Swimming _____
Tennis _____
Golf _____
Dancing _____
Airplane Travel _____
Liquor intake _____
Other _____
_____

Do you consider fetal movements as very active _____ passive _____ or average _____?
Other Unusual Behavior and Influences _____
_____
_____
_____
_____
_____
_____
_____
_____

RECORD 3   Recorder _____

Record of Birth

EDITOR'S NOTE Birth is the best time to begin a lifetime record. Through the process of joyfully tracking your baby's progress you will create a unique product—a detailed, personal, and informative record of your baby. This is useful in itself, but the Princeton Center for Infancy (PCI) attaches equal value to the process itself. Keeping records will increase your confidence in being able to read your infant's signals and at the same time sensitize you to the real expert on infant growth and development—your baby!

Named for _____

Birth date _____ at _____ o'clock   Birth sign _____

Place _____
                           Home or Hospital Name

Address _____
           Street   City   State   Zip

Sex _____   Weight at Birth _____   Hair Color _____   Skin Color _____

Length (inches) _____   Eye Color _____   Birth Order (1st, 2nd child etc.) _____

Personal physician _____
                    Name   Address   City and State

In-house doctor _____
                    Name   Address   City and State

Nurses _____

Baby "Roomed-in" _____   Circumcision _____

Father present _____   Childbirth preparation _____

Other pertinent data (describe prenatal courses taken, number of sessions, whether father attended) _____
_____
_____

Left hospital on _____   Feeding: Breast _____   Other _____

Weight _____ lbs. _____ oz.   Remarks _____

Formula _____   Remarks _____

Religious ceremony _____   Baptized: Yes _____ No _____

Godfather _____   Godmother _____

Others present _____
_____
_____

RECORD 4   Recorder _____   21

Record of Adoption

EDITOR'S NOTE Years ago the phrase "Give me a child before he is five," emphasized the fact that by five, a child's personality is fixed. Today psychologists place the formative period more nearly at the first three months of life. The early months of every infant are vital to his or her physical well-being, emotional security, and establishment of social attachments. Adoptive parents should try to get their baby as early as possible.

Date of adoption _____ Age at adoption _____ Where _____
How adopted _____
_____
_____

Biological parents' history (if available) _____
_____
_____
_____

Prior foster parents _____
_____
_____
_____

Early pre-adoption behavior _____
_____
_____
_____

Other _____
_____
_____
_____
_____

RECORD 5

Photographic Record of Birth or Adoption

Picture at Birth or Adoption

Picture at Birth or Adoption

Picture of Family or Religious Ceremony

Other

RECORD 6   23

Identification Marks on Newborn

EDITOR'S NOTE *Any two of these marks will serve as identification for your baby. Attach other hospital identification material here. If space is insufficient, take record into any Xerox or other copy center for a one-third reduction. Then glue or staple to this record. (Keep in a manila envelope other keepsakes, such as hospital bracelet.)*

                        Birthmarks   Baby's footprints
             (Give location and diagram
               to indicate size and shape.)

                 Baby's palmprints

                                                       Baby's ear identification

           Mother's right index finger   Photo at Birth

RECORD 7   Recorder _____   24

First Day of Life – Hospital Chart
(A Professional Record)

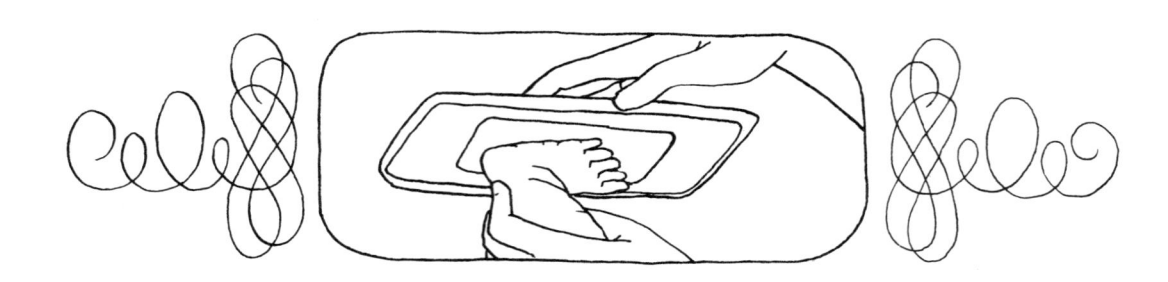

EDITOR'S NOTE *This information should be obtained from baby's chart before leaving the hospital. Have doctor or nurse fill in chart or this record. What takes place before and at the time of birth may affect future health care. It also helps a doctor or hospital to find the birth and hospital record. The blood group determined at birth remains the same throughout life and should be recorded.*

Child's Name _____ Date _____

Apgar Score: Developed by the late Dr. Virginia Apgar, it is a quick check at birth of respiration, muscle tone, reflexes, heart rate, and color. It serves to alert doctors if a baby needs special attention. It also can be a clue to difficulties the child might have later in life.

Apgar Score at 1 minute _____ at 5 minutes _____

Name, address, and hospital affiliation _____

_____

Obstetrician _____

Anesthetist _____

Pediatrician _____

Treatment, if indicated _____

Resuscitator _____ Oxygen _____ Vitamin K _____

Incubator—amount of time _____ hours _____ days

Baby's blood group _____ Type _____ Rh Factor (circle one) Positive or Negative

Transfusions: Simple _____ Exchange _____

RECORD 7 (CONTINUED)

Bilirubin: A blood test (used when there is jaundice) that provides the physician with an indication of the effectiveness of treatment. (Bilirubin is one of the pigments produced in the destruction of red blood cells.)

Direct _____   Indirect _____

_____

_____

PKU (Phenylketonuria): A blood test that should be administered to all newborns. (It is required by law in most states.) Blood is taken from the baby's heel twenty-four hours after the first protein feeding before the baby leaves the hospital. The condition is a hereditary deficiency. Treatment is fully effective; untreated, it causes mental retardation. _____

_____

_____

If baby is born prematurely, fill out this information:

Hospital _____   How long _____

Exposure to oxygen _____   How long _____

Tests (describe) _____

Other information on follow-up (clinics, etc.) _____

_____

_____

_____

_____

_____

_____

_____

RECORD 8   Recorder _____   26

Medical Examination at Birth

(TO BE FILLED OUT BY EXAMINING DOCTOR AT BIRTH)
(A Professional Record)

EDITOR'S NOTE Have the obstetrician and/or pediatrician or hospital doctor fill in this record. You may have trouble getting a busy doctor to fill it out. Try anyway! If you cannot get any co-operation, ask the nurse to fill it out. If she or he is too busy, have a copy made and leave it to be filled out by the doctor at his or her leisure.

Private Doctor _____
　　　　　　　　Name　　　　　　　　　　　　　　Address

_____
　　　　　　City, State, Zip　　　　　　　　　　　　　　　Telephone

Hospital's Name _____ Address _____

Hospital Doctor _____

Date _____ Name of Newborn _____

General Appearance at Birth _____

Weight _____ Height _____ Color of Eyes _____ Hair Color _____

Head Circumference _____ Chest Circumference _____

Temperature (rectal) _____ Color of Fingers and Toes _____

Respiration Rate _____ Pulse Rate _____

Breathing Patterns (times per minute) High _____ Low _____ Labored _____

Baby's Cry: Vigorous _____ Weak _____ Facial Muscles _____ Color _____

Movement of 4 Limbs _____

Reaction to Labor: Exhausted _____ Disorganized _____ Sleepy _____

　Sucking well _____ Interest in Feeding _____ Breast or Bottle _____

Effect of Drugs on Baby (taken by mother as pain reliever) _____

　Alert _____ Slowed down _____

Head

Normal _____

Forcep Marks _____

Fontanelles _____

Sutures _____

Bruises _____

Caput Succedaneum _____

Cephalohematoma _____

RECORD 8 (CONTINUED)

Eyes

Normal _____

Cataract _____

Discharge _____

Hemorrhage _____

Jaundice _____

Other _____

Cornea: Clear _____ Cloudy _____

Pupils: Size _____ Reaction _____

Nystagmus _____ Strabismus _____

Drugs Administered

Oxygen _____ How long _____ Amount _____

Silver Nitrate _____

Other _____

Nose

Normal _____ General shape _____ Breathing in Both Nostrils _____

Abnormal _____ Blockage in Back of Nose _____ Sneezing (reaction to powder) _____

Ears (auditory screening if available)

Normal _____ Abnormal _____

Mouth and Throat

Normal _____

Palate _____ Lips _____ Gums _____

Tongue _____ Born with Tooth? _____

Frenulum _____ Short _____ Long _____

Infections _____

Other _____

Neck

Normal _____ Abnormal _____

Swellings _____

Torticollis _____

Size of Thyroid Gland _____

Other _____

RECORD 8 (CONTINUED)

Face

Normal _____

Abnormal _____

Cardiac Pulmonary System — Chest

Normal _____

Abnormal _____

Heart Rate, Rhythm, Sounds _____

Respiratory Rate, Rhythm, Sounds _____

Murmurs _____

Femoral Pulse (in groin) _____

Other _____

Abdomen

Normal _____

Distension _____

Hernia _____

Palpable Kidney, Liver, Spleen _____

Umbilical Granuloma _____

_____

_____

Umbilical Cord: How it was cut _____

Other _____

Rectum and Anus

Normal _____

Fissures _____

Other _____

Genitals Male _____ Female _____

Normal _____ Normal _____

Hernia _____ Adhesions _____

Hydrocele _____ Discharge _____

Phimosis _____ Edema _____

Testes Descended _____ Hernia _____

Circumcision _____ Other _____

Other _____ _____

RECORD 8 (CONTINUED)

Muscular Skeletal System

Normal _____

Flaccidity _____ Deformities _____

Paralysis _____ Gluteal Creases _____

Spasticity _____ Moro Reflex _____ Fractures _____

Other _____

Spine

Normal _____

Curvature _____ **Dislocation (partial or complete)** _____

Other _____

Skin

Normal _____

Birthmarks _____ Desquamation _____

Scalp _____ Eruption _____

Syanosis (blue) _____ Pallor _____ Jaundice _____

Other _____

Feeding

Breast _____ Formula (type) _____

_____

_____

Reflexes (rate plus or minus)

rooting _____ moro _____ step _____ grasp _____ response to touch _____

Additional Medical Information

_____   _____
_____   _____
_____   _____
_____   _____

_____
_____
_____
_____

Examining Doctor's Name _____ Address _____

City, State, Zip _____ Telephone _____

RECORD 9

Valuable Documents and Photos

EDITOR'S NOTE Many documents are created in these earliest months that can serve your child's best interests throughout life. A birth certificate, record of immunizations, and early photos will be essential for attending school and later for running for public office, obtaining passports, inheriting property, and even insuring a pension for the parents. If the birth certificate is too large, ask a Xerox or other copy center for a one-third reduction.*

BIRTH CERTIFICATE

Attach copy of birth certificate here.
(Order one from State Vital Statistics Office.
Ask hospital for address and procedure.)

Birth Certificate No. _____ Recorded at _____
                                                           Place and Date

*Copy centers usually have copiers that can reduce a birth certificate by one-third or two-thirds at $.15 to $.20 extra. If you cannot locate a birth certificate or lack one, the U.S. Bureau of the Census can document your age (not your birth date) via the census taken after your birth. The transcript is acceptable to federal and state agencies and virtually all of private industry. For $7.50 you can have two censuses searched and a transcript sent to you or your child. Write for a form to the Personal Census Service Branch, Bureau of the Census, Pittsburg, KS 66762.

RECORD 9 (CONTINUED)

Photograph

Photograph

Baby's First Day

Father and Mother

Photograph

Baby's First Home

RECORD 10   Recorder _____

Feeding in Infancy

EDITOR'S NOTE Eating should be a pleasant and matter-of-fact experience. In the first year, feeding satisfies the essential needs for growth and survival. A baby's birth weight is tripled by the first birthday. During the second year, interest in food and appetite fall off sharply and play second fiddle to a toddler's drive toward self-feeding, self-help, and independence (I eat by myself!).

	Breast	*Bottle*
Sucking	Milk came in _____ day	First bottle _____ day
	Breast-fed baby from _____ to _____ wks.	Bottle-fed baby from _____ to _____ wks.
	Baby at each breast _____ min.	Formula used. Enriched formula, if any _____
	Occasional bottle _____	_____
	Date introduced _____	_____
	Which feeding _____	
	Comments _____	

Duration of Feeding   *On Demand*   Number of minutes _____
                                             Number of hours between feeding _____
                    On Schedule   Number of minutes _____
                                               Number of hours between feeding _____

Check which best describes your child

Burping	Hiccoughs _____	Comments _____
	Back-patting burper _____	_____
	Stomach-on-lap burper _____	_____
	Sitting-on-lap burper _____	_____

Night Feeding   Frequency _____ Nightly from _____ to _____ wks.
                      Frequency _____ Nightly from _____ to _____ wks.
                      Sleeps through the night at age _____
                                                     (wks. and days)

RECORD 10 (CONTINUED)

Allergies   Is your baby allergic to milk? What was done about it? _____
_____

List foods that caused an allergic reaction _____
_____

Feeding Utensils   Fed from spoon at _____ mos.   Sat at family table at _____ mos.
and Equipment   Drank from cup at _____ mos.   Other feeding accomplishments
                    Sat in infant seat at _____ mos.   _____
                    Sat in high chair at _____ mos.   _____
                    Sat at feeding table at _____ mos. _____

Self-feeding   Held bottle at age _____   Used spoon at age _____
(in mos.)   Held cup at age _____   Three meals established at age _____
                Finger foods at age _____

Solid Foods   Did you prepare your own baby foods (check) _____ or use
               commercially prepared foods? (check) _____
               On which foods did your child become hooked?

               _____ _____ _____ _____
               _____ _____ _____ _____
               _____ _____ _____ _____

Feeding Problems   Dawdler _____   Plays with food _____
                    "No want!" _____   Wails for snacks _____
                    Comments _____
                    _____

Other Feeding Notes _____
_____
_____
_____
_____
_____
_____

RECORD 11

Medical Check-ups

EDITOR'S NOTE Use these records and make up additional ones when you take your baby in for monthly check-ups. Jot down questions and doctor's answers and recommendations.

Date _____ Recorder _____

Physician _____ Address _____

Place of Exam _____ Date of Exam _____

Baby's Age _____ Weight _____ Height _____

Your Questions _____
_____
_____

Doctor's Recommendations _____
_____
_____

Your Comments _____
_____
_____

Date _____ Recorder _____

Physician _____ Address _____

Place of Exam _____ Date of Exam _____

Baby's Age _____ Weight _____ Height _____

Your Questions _____
_____
_____

Doctor's Recommendations _____
_____
_____

Your Comments _____
_____
_____

RECORD 11 (CONTINUED)

- -

Date _____ Recorder _____

Physician _____ Address _____

Place of Exam _____ Date of Exam _____

Child's Age _____ Weight _____ Height _____

Your Questions _____

_____

_____

Doctor's Recommendations _____

_____

_____

Your Comments _____

_____

_____

- -

Date _____ Recorder _____

Physician _____ Address _____

Place of Exam _____ Date of Exam _____

Child's Age _____ Weight _____ Height _____

Your Questions _____

_____

_____

Doctor's Recommendations _____

_____

_____

Your Comments _____

_____

_____

RECORD 12   Recorder _____

Height and Growth Chart

EDITOR'S NOTE Height is one of the few genetically determined traits. Except for good nutrition, the environmental factors are negligible. Since your parenting role here is minor, sit back and enjoy your little one's growth spurts and plateaus. Some months she seems "to grow like a weed"; other times there is no apparent growth.

How tall is baby's Father _____ Mother _____ Paternal Grandfather _____
Sister _____ Brother _____ Paternal Grandmother _____
Brother _____ Sister _____ Maternal Grandfather _____
Maternal Grandmother _____

Average Height for Girls (in inches)	Age	*Average Height for Boys* (in inches)	Age	*Your Child's Height*
24½	3-6 months	25½	Birth	_____
26¾	6-9 months	27½	1 Month	_____
28¾	9-12 months	29¾	6 Months	_____
30¾	1-1½ years	31	1 Year	_____
32	1½-2 years	33¼	1½ Years	_____
35	2 years	36	2 Years	_____
38½	3 years	39	2½ Years	_____
41¾	4 years	42	3 Years	_____
44	5 years	44	4 Years	_____
46	6 years	46¾	5 Years	_____
48	7 years	49	6 Years	_____
50¾	8 years	51	7 Years	_____
53¼	9 years	53¼	8 Years	_____
55½	10 years	55¼	9 Years	_____
58½	11 years	57¼	10 Years	_____
60½	12 years	59	11 Years	_____
61¼	13 years	61	12 Years	_____
			13 Years	_____
			14 Years	_____
			15 Years	_____
			16 Years	_____

RECORD 12 (CONTINUED)

EDITOR'S NOTE Pediatricians suggest using this type of chart to record the height of your child. Put dots on the proper intersection and graph your child's height increase every year.

CHILD'S HEIGHT CHART

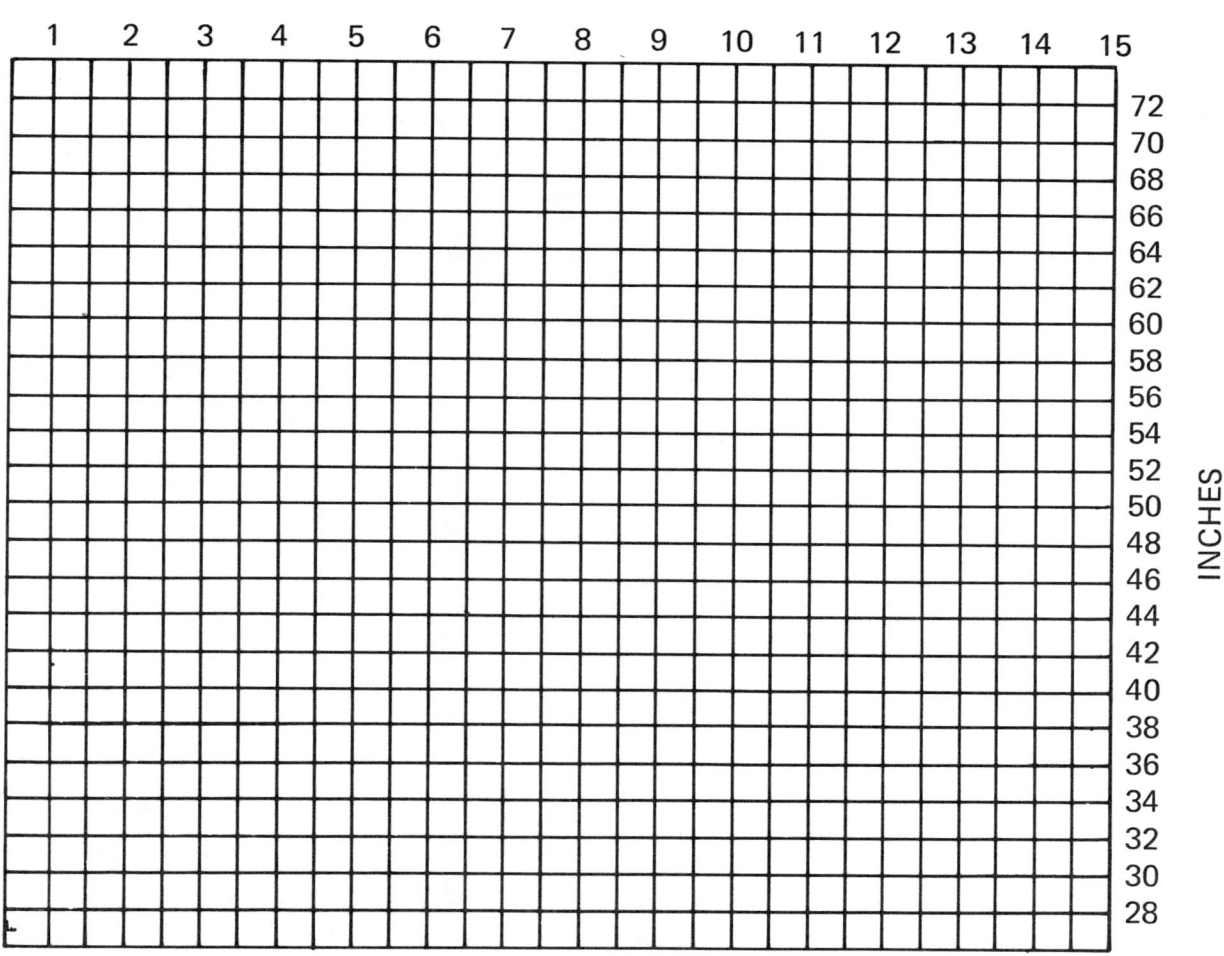

YEARS / INCHES

RECORD 13   Recorder _____   38

Weight and Growth Chart

EDITOR'S NOTE *With respect to weight, life is not so rosy! The most recent research suggests "you are what you eat" and goes on to shatter the idyllic myth of the chubby, contented, overfed baby. Fat babies make for overweight adults and are medically a high-risk group. This is one area where the Princeton Center for Infancy urges parents to heed norms and averages. The statistics will provide you with limits you may follow with your baby. With your doctor's help, establish sensible, appropriate, nutritious diets. <u>This is especially important in the first two years of life</u>.*

Average Weight for Girls	Age	Average Weight for Boys	Age	Your Child's Weight
14½ pounds	3-6 months	16 pounds	Birth	_____
18½ pounds	6-9 months	19¾ pounds	1 Month	_____
20½ pounds	9-12 months	22½ pounds	3 Months	_____
23½ pounds	1-1½ years	24¼ pounds	6 Months	_____
24¾ pounds	1½-2 years	27 pounds	9 Months	_____
29 pounds	2 years	30½ pounds	12 Months	_____
33¼ pounds	3 years	34¾ pounds	2 Years	_____
38¾ pounds	4 years	39¾ pounds	3 Years	_____
42½ pounds	5 years	44½ pounds	4 Years	_____
47½ pounds	6 years	48½ pounds	5 Years	_____
53½ pounds	7 years	54½ pounds	6 Years	_____
60¾ pounds	8 years	61¼ pounds	8 Years	_____
69 pounds	9 years	69 pounds	10 Years	_____
77 pounds	10 years	74½ pounds	12 Years	_____
87½ pounds	11 years	85 pounds	14 Years	_____
94 pounds	12 years	89 pounds	16 Years	_____
103 pounds	13 years	99 pounds		

RECORD 14   Recorder _____   39

The Newborn's Reflexes

EDITOR'S NOTE Newborns are not as helpless as they look. From the first moment, they can breathe, suck, swallow, and eliminate wastes; they hear, smell, see shadows (six to seven inches away), and taste.

Physically, however, newborns are very limited. With a head that is two thirds of their height, and legs and arms half their size, they need help. Fortunately, this problem was worked out by Mother Nature. Spontaneous, automatic reflexes beyond their control take over in these earliest months and serve their needs well. Before you develop unwarranted fears (because of the jerky movements at loud sounds, flailing of limbs, and so on), it would be well to check out these reflexes for yourself and watch them undergo "extinction" (when they are no longer needed for survival). Discover how purposeful and intentional behavior takes over. As the movements come under control of the cortex of the brain (movements of eyes, mouth, fingers, legs) and as the baby's nervous system becomes better organized, she is no longer merely reactive to stimuli. She starts making active demands on the environment (people, things, etc.). The infant's behavior becomes intentional, not reflexive. If your baby does not express actions described on the pages that follow, it may not indicate the disorder listed, but the facts should be called to the attention of the doctor.

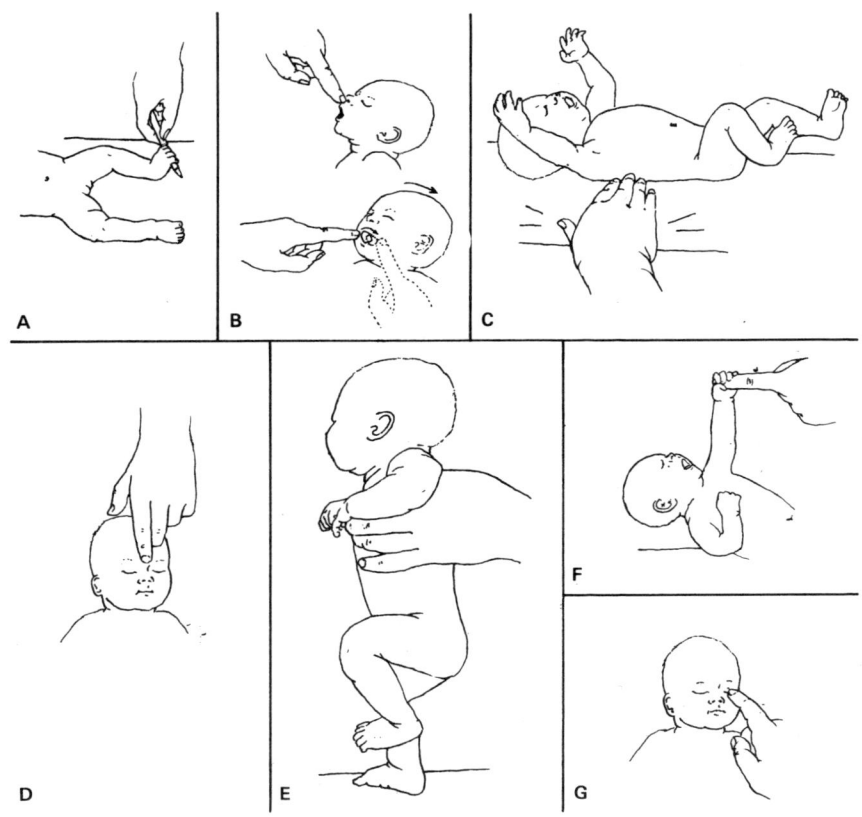

RECORD 14 (CONTINUED)

Reflex	How Tested. If you:	Then Baby's:	Age When First Noticed
Toe Grasp (Plantar) A	place finger (or pencil) under toes	toes grasp by flexing	_____
Righting Reflex (not shown)	put baby on tummy on flat surface	head turns to side; baby lifts self with arms and "crawls"	_____
Babinski (not shown)	stroke sole of foot at base of digits, from heel to toe (using knitting needle)	toes grasp needle and flex. Toes spread; large toe sticks up.	_____
Rooting B	stroke corner of mouth, moving finger toward cheek (baby must be awake)	mouth roots, head turns, and tongue moves to stroking object	_____
Moro (Startle) Reflex C	bang suddenly on table or side of crib	arms are sharply extended	_____
Blink (Pupillary) (not shown)	shine flashlight	eyes close tightly	_____
Nasopalpebral D	tap bridge of nose with finger or cotton	eyes close tightly	_____
Stepping E	support infant under armpits to stand	feet engage in rhythmic "walking" movements	_____
Automatic Hand Grasp (Palmar) F	press rod or finger against palm of hand	hand grasps rod or finger; can be lifted off table	_____
Withdrawal Reflex (not shown)	lightly prick soles of feet	knee and foot flex, withdrawal takes place	_____
Ciliary Reflex G	touch an eyelid	eye will blink	_____

RECORD 14 (CONTINUED)

Age When It Disappeared	Age When It Should Disappear or Persist	Significance of Its Continuation
_____	9 to 12 months	Continuance may indicate immaturity of nervous system.
_____	Persists	Absence suggests dysfunction of nervous system.
_____	12 to 18 months. Replaced by flex of big toes as in adulthood.	If absent, may indicate a problem in nervous system.
_____	9 to 12 months	In retarded children, it may be active for years.
_____	disappears at 4 to 6 months	Continuation after 6 months may indicate immaturity of nervous system.
_____	Persists	Failure to appear may indicate a visual problem. Discuss it with your doctor.
_____	Disappears in first few months of life	Failure to appear may indicate a visual difficulty. Discuss it with your doctor.
_____	2 to 4 months	Not a good indicator of any abnormality or normal growth.
_____	5 to 6 months	Reflexes replaced by voluntary grasp (4-6 months). Lack of voluntary grasp may be a problem in sitting, standing.
_____	Gone before child walks (9 to 12 months)	Absence may indicate nerve damage.
_____	Persists into adulthood	

First Twelve Months

MASTERING MOTOR AND SENSORY POWERS

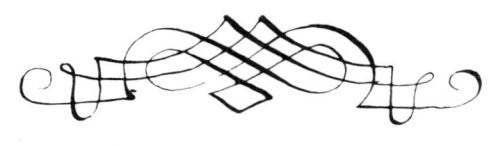

FIRST TWELVE MONTHS OF LIFE

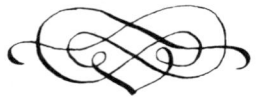

RECORD 15   Recorder _____

Growth and Development–
First Twelve Months of Life

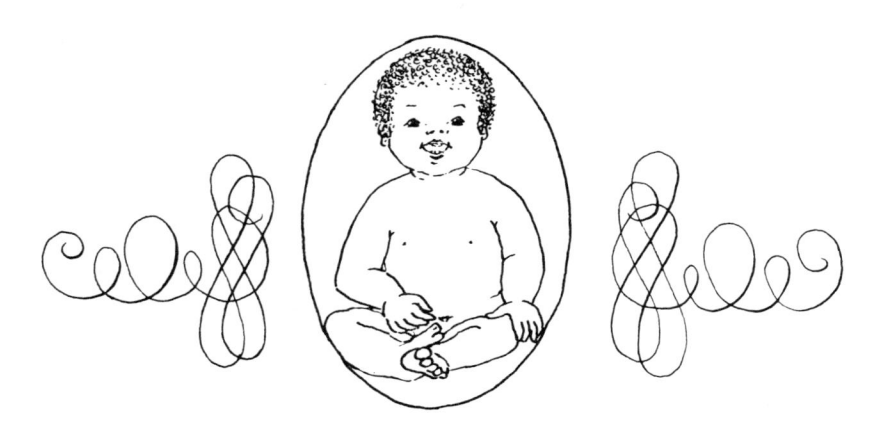

EDITOR'S NOTE So many different physical, social, and emotional changes occur so rapidly in this period that few parents can recognize the "ages and stages" of an infant's growth. From a passive, helpless being who had to be fed about six times a day and night, flailing hands and feet endlessly, your baby will have mastered seeing, hearing, fingering, grasping, reaching, sitting, crawling, standing, creeping and, in some cases, walking, running, and climbing. When she reaches her first birthday, she will have established trust in you, learned how to smile and laugh with you, given as well as taken affection, understood most of your commands. Under your tutelage, she has learned how to function in the world of people, space, and things.

Basic Measurements

Weight at 12 months _____ Height at 12 months _____ Shoe Size _____ Clothing size _____

Large-Muscle Control
(specify in months when mastered)

Holds head upright _____

Turns over _____

Creeps _____

Crawls _____

Stands alone _____

Squats _____

Sits down _____

Walks _____

Climbs up and down stairs _____

Small-Muscle Control
(specify in months when mastered)

Holds object _____

Holds bottle _____

Picks up tiny objects with thumb and forefinger _____

Removes cover from jar _____

Carries spoon to mouth _____

Pulls _____

Pushes _____

RECORD 15 (CONTINUED)

Language Development
(specify onset in months)

Cooing _____

Vocal-social response to mother's smile
_____

Begins babbling, experimenting with sound
_____

Recognizes name _____

Vocalizes pleasure or displeasure _____

Imitates sound or sound sequence _____

Understands and obeys command _____

Names several objects _____

Sensory Responses
(specify onset in months)

Follows moving object with eyes and head
_____

Pulls dangling object _____

Carries object to mouth _____

Picks up block on contact _____

Reaches and grasps toy with one hand
_____

Distinguishes near and far objects _____

Grasps, manipulates, mouths _____

Fears heights _____

Mental and Cognitive Growth
(specify onset in months)

Looks for hidden toys _____

Looks for toys that disappear _____

Imitates adult actions _____

Responds to mirror image _____

Discriminates parents and siblings from others
_____

Identifies body parts _____

Uses one hand to hold, other hand to
explore _____

Favorite games with parents _____
_____
_____
_____
_____

Favorite songs and recordings _____
_____
_____
_____

Social Growth
(specify onset in months)

Shows fear, disgust, and anger _____

Initiates play _____

Has toy preference _____

Protects self and possessions _____

Establishes meaning of "no" _____

Helps dress self _____

Holds cup _____

Gives affection to humans _____

RECORD 15 (CONTINUED)

Favorite playthings _____
_____
_____
_____
_____

Describe relations with siblings (brothers and sisters) and other adults if members of household
_____
_____
_____
_____
_____
_____
_____

First birthday (where and how celebrated) _____
_____
_____
_____
_____

Favorite gifts _____
_____
_____

Memories of first year of life _____
_____
_____
_____
_____
_____

RECORD 16

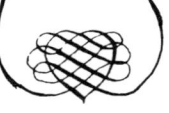

Photographic Record

Photos of
First 12 months

RECORD 17   Recorder _____

Hearing Test – Birth to Eight Months

EDITOR'S NOTE *Most audiologists and many pediatricians believe that all newborns should be given a hearing test, and that such an evaluation should include a brief history of observation by parents, and a genetic history of deafness in the family (grandparents, cousins, etc.). No age is too young for detection. Any reported slight hearing loss should be followed up periodically throughout the first five years in every visit to a doctor. If there is continued loss of hearing, ask your doctor to refer you to an audiologist. There are 3.5 million births a year, and 3,000 babies are deaf at birth. There are other degrees of deafness that show up later because of genetic factors (inheritance) and parental diseases (maternal rubella, Rh Negative mother, etc.). These would never come to the attention of audiologists if parents did not help in the detection. We present a typical questionnaire for you to fill out and refer to your doctor for attention.*

Parent Questionnaire

(Answer *Yes* if you have very definitely seen your child do these things even once or twice. If you have never seen her do them, answer *No*.)*

Yes   No   *Birth to four months*

____   ____   1. Does your baby startle to a sudden sound, such as a cough, a shout, a dog bark, or a handclap? (Discount responses to a door slamming, the stamp of a foot, a loud airplane or truck noise, and other vibrations.)

____   ____   2. When sleeping in a quiet room, does your infant stir or awaken when someone speaks, or a noise is made near him? (Some babies used to noisy surroundings may ignore these interruptions.)

____   ____   3. When crying or fretful, does your baby appear to calm down, even momentarily, when you speak out of eyeshot, or when music starts up, or when a sudden loud noise occurs?

____   ____   4. At 3 to 4 months, does your infant occasionally seem to make a feeble head turn toward a sound or move her eyes in its direction?

                Four to eight months

____   ____   1. Does your baby turn his head and eyes in the direction of a sound that is out of his peripheral vision? (At 4 months, the infant should begin to turn directly to the side.)

____   ____   2. In a quiet situation, does your baby change expression or widen her eyes when hearing a fairly loud sound or voice?

____   ____   3. By 6 months, does your baby seem to talk or bable to persons in response to their speaking or making sounds?

____   ____   4. Does your infant briefly enjoy ringing bells, squeezing noisemakers?

*If you have answered *No* to any of the above questions, your baby's hearing should be checked.

RECORD 18   Recorder _____

Vision Record at Five Months

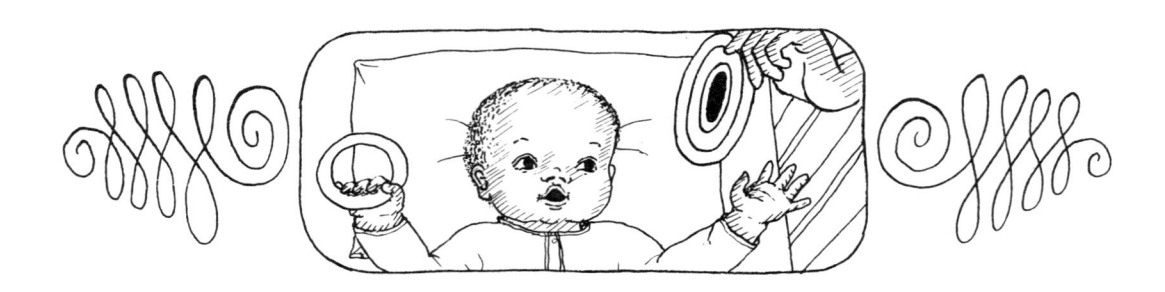

EDITOR'S NOTE *During the earliest months of life your baby is greatly unco-ordinated, but is receptive to sensory stimulation and looking at his surroundings for most of his waking hours. Newborns react to light intensity, patterns, and color. They stare intently at a face several inches away. This is the time to start checking visual development.*

Factors at Birth (supplied by attending physician):

Prophylactic for infection administered

Silver nitrate _____ other _____

Oxygen administered _____ how long _____ amount _____

Conjunctiva (pale or infected) _____ Ocular position and movement _____

_____ Cornea (clear or cloudy) _____

Pupils (size, reaction) _____ Eyegrounds (fundi) and media _____

Vision, Movement and Balance (as observed by parents; indicate ages observed):

First real tears _____ Looks at bright light _____

Inspects own hand in play _____ Reaches for and grasps objects _____

Eyes move together to follow _____ moving objects _____ light _____ large bright objects

Tracking (indicate ages observed and object used):

a light _____ a puff of breath _____

8" away _____ 2' away _____

faces _____ plain objects _____ stripes or bull's-eye _____

Color preference: white _____ fluorescent yellow _____

Looks longer at red _____ gray _____

RECORD 18 (CONTINUED)

Problems noted (if any of these conditions exist, consult an eye physician):

crossed eyes (if persistent) _____

limitation of movement of eyes or lids _____

constant tearing, discharge and redness _____

cloudiness of cornea or pupil _____

Examination by ophthalmologist or optometrist Dr. _____ date _____

Eye examination by attending doctor is advisable: *

at birth: for inspection of birth defects.

at 6 months: for diagnosis of any persistent or marked deviation of one eye.

at 1 year: for diagnosis of co-ordinated movements of both eyes without deviation of one eye.

at 3-4 years: for testing of visual acuity and muscle co-ordination.

at 6 years (before entering school): for testing visual acuity.

at any age: if problems are observed.

(Note: Screening tests for visual acuity detect not only poorly focused images in farsightedness, etc., but also poor function caused by any other abnormality or disease.)

- -

Examination: Dr. _____ Date _____

Findings _____

Treatment _____

Progress _____

_____

_____

_____

- -

Examination: Dr. _____ Date _____

Findings _____

Treatment _____

Progress _____

_____

_____

_____

*See Record 38

RECORD 19   Recorder _____

*Immunization Schedule**

EDITOR'S NOTE The American Academy of Pediatrics recommends that children be immunized and given the tuberculin test according to the immunization schedule below. Vaccine schedules and combinations are constantly being improved. Therefore, <u>consult your physician for exact and latest variations</u>. Record month and year each immunization was completed and any special reactions that occurred.

Baby's Age	Name of Inoculation	Name of Disease To Be Resisted	Date Received, Parents Comments (describe reaction)
2 mos.	DTP Vaccine	Diphtheria, Tetanus, Pertussis (whooping cough)	_____
	Polio Vaccine (first dose)	Polio	_____
4 mos.	DTP Vaccine (second shot)	Diphtheria, etc., as above	_____
	Polio Vaccine (completed)	Polio	_____
6 mos.	DTP Vaccine (completed)	Diptheria, etc., as above	_____
12 mos.	Tuberculin Test	Tuberculosis	_____
15 mos.	Measles Vaccine Mumps Vaccine Rubella	Red Measles Mumps German Measles	_____
18 mos.	DTP Booster	Diphtheria, etc., as above	_____
4 to 6 yrs.	DTP	Diphtheria etc., as above	_____
	Polio Vaccine	Polio	_____
14 to 16 yrs.	Combined Tetanus and Diphtheria (adult type)	Tetanus, Diphtheria	_____

*Schedule revised in 1977 by Amer. Academy of Pediatrics.

RECORD 19 (CONTINUED)

Vaccination Against Other Diseases
As new vaccines (flu, etc.) are discovered, you will want your child to be immunized and to record name of vaccines, date, and doctor's name (or clinic).

Age	Name of Inoculation	Name of Diseases To Be Resisted	Doctor, Date, Observations, Reaction, Comments

Comments _____

RECORD 20   Recorder _____

Sleep Patterns in First Year

EDITOR'S NOTE *During the first year your baby will be asleep a good bit of the time. In general, sleep patterns follow a typical sequence: the younger baby sleeps lightly, a great deal and fitfully; the older baby has fewer sleep periods, sleeps deeply and quietly for a longer period of time.*

Sleeping Place:

During Infancy: basket or bassinet _____   cradle _____
                  crib _____   carriage _____
                  in own room _____   in parents' room _____

Preparation (note ages):

During the Day: special blanket _____   music box _____
                  pacifier _____   is sung to _____
                  sucks finger _____   shades drawn _____
                  sucks thumb _____   quiet area _____
                                                   other _____

At Night: bath _____   rocking _____
                  night bottle _____   lights out _____
                  patting _____   change of clothing _____
                                                   other _____

Length of Uninterrupted Sleep (average estimates: 3½ hrs. at birth, 9½ hrs. at 1 yr.):

0-3 mos. _____   6-9 mos. _____

3-6 mos. _____   9-12 mos. _____

RECORD 20 (CONTINUED)

Number of Sleep Periods (average estimates: 12 periods at birth, 6 periods at 1 yr.):

0-3 mos. _____   6-9 mos. _____

3-6 mos. _____   9-12 mos. _____

Preferred Sleep Position (most infants assume the fetal position):

0-3 mos. _____   6-9 mos. _____

3-6 mos. _____   9-12 mos. _____

Signs of Fatigue (newborns yawn; 3-month-old babies slowly open and close eyelids; older babies' movements become uncertain and slow):

0-3 mos. _____   6-9 mos. _____

3-6 mos. _____   9-12 mos. _____

Other Comments _____
_____
_____
_____
_____
_____
_____
_____
_____
_____
_____
_____
_____
_____
_____
_____

RECORD 21   Recorder _____   56

Early Behavior Record – First to Third Months
(A Researcher's Record)

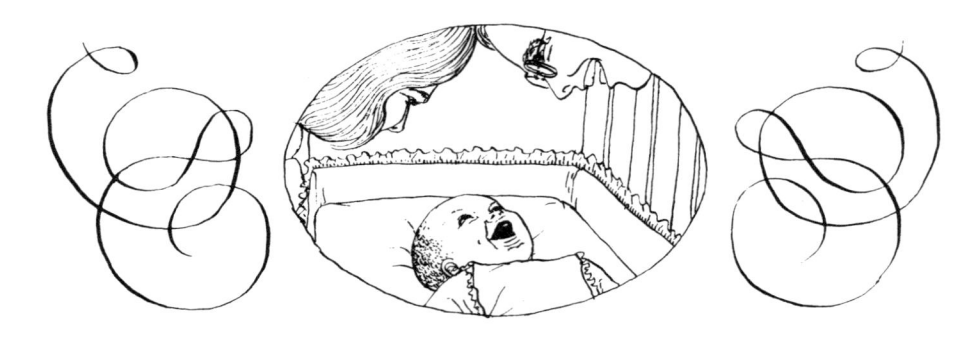

EDITOR'S NOTE *Babies are not alike at birth either physically or psychologically. They have their own unique behavioral styles, and the quicker you identify your baby's special temperament (mild-mannered, intense, changeable, etc.), the easier life will be for the entire family. Don't make the mistake of typecasting your new baby as passive. Don't short-change your baby by not providing suitable physical and sensory stimulation.*

Crying: a great deal _____ little _____ none _____
Afternoon fussiness: onset _____ ended _____ degree (*high, average, low*) _____
Sleeping: amount (in a 24-hr. period) _____
Feeding (sucking action): enthusiastic _____ passive _____

Baby's responsiveness to (note preference and dates of onset in weeks and days)

parent's touch _____	extending tongue (in response to parent's tongue extending) _____
parent's play _____	
a smile (first) _____	Other _____
patting or stroking _____	_____
humming, singing _____	_____
looking at a mirror _____	_____

Baby initiates interaction (note dates in weeks and days of onset)

first smile _____	vocalizes _____
cough game _____	cries to obtain something _____
	Other _____

RECORD 21 (CONTINUED)

Temperament: This trait may be identified according to several behavioral criteria suggested below. Most researchers believe that basic temperament is inherited and fairly stable. Rate baby *high*, *average* or *low*.

Level of activity (active baby moves constantly, even in sleep) _____
_____
_____
_____

Rhythmicity (some babies have built-in alarm clocks; others are totally unpredictable as to hunger, sleep, etc.) _____
_____
_____
_____

Sensory (some babies startle easily, show strong preferences for certain clothing, react to light, etc.; others do not) _____
_____
_____
_____

Response to pain (amount of energy displayed in responding: some babies howl, others fuss and fidget softly) _____
_____
_____
_____

Distractability (some concentrate better than others) _____
_____
_____
_____

Persistence (ability to "stick with it") _____
_____
_____
_____
_____
_____
_____

RECORD 22   Recorder _____

Visual-motor Skills

EDITOR'S NOTE During the first six months of life, your baby will develop several visual-motor functions: visually directed reaching, visual attention, visual accommodation, and blinking. Record your baby's progress, using this chart. Note the dates of onset and other observations.

Ability	Newborn-2 months	2-4 months*	4-6 months
VISUAL ATTENTION (that state when infant's eyes are more than half open)			

Parent's Comments _____

_____

_____

_____

_____

_____

_____

_____

_____

Ability	Newborn-2 months[†]	2-4 months[‡]	4-6 months
VISUAL ACCOMMODATION (seeing ability)			

Parent's Comments _____

_____

_____

_____

_____

_____

_____

_____

_____

*Expect marked increase due to discovery of hands at 2 months.   [†]Child can see only at distance of 7" between eye and object.
[‡]By the end of the 4th month, visual ability is like an adult's.

RECORD 22 (CONTINUED)

Ability	Newborn-2 months	2-4 months	4-6 months
BLINKING RESPONSE (defined as rapidly closing and opening eyes due to increased air pressure or physical target coming near)	Usually matures by end of 2nd month		

Parent's Comments _____
_____
_____
_____
_____
_____
_____
_____

Ability	Newborn-2 months	2-4 months	4-6 months**
FOOT REACHING	Reflex behavior		

Parent's Comments _____
_____
_____
_____
_____
_____
_____
_____

**By now, feet are used to move objects, turn toys, push bumpers.

RECORD 23   Recorder _____   60

Developing the Senses

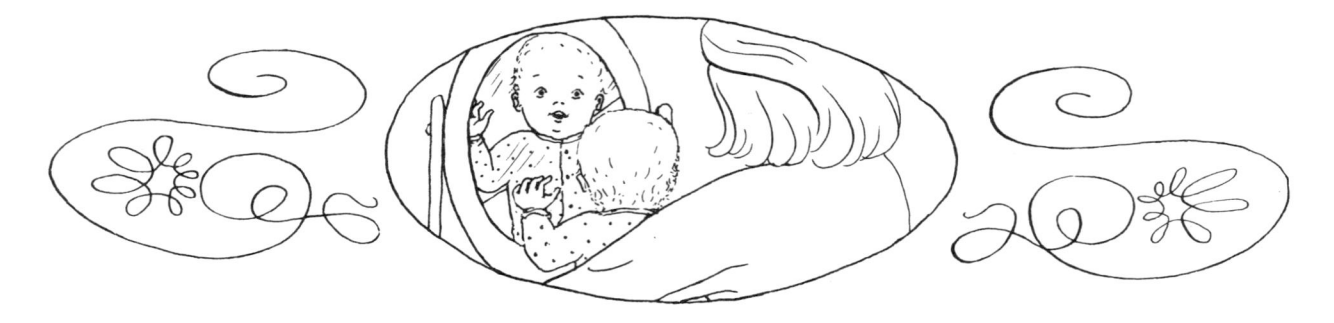

EDITOR'S NOTE All babies taste, smell, and hear at birth. They see well at six weeks, finger and touch from six to twelve weeks, kick with intention at twelve to twenty weeks. As these sensory powers mature there is a strong desire to practice them. Parents or care-givers can enrich the very young child's world with sense experiences, using things around the house. Try to find these items and record your infant's experiences. Or make a set or your own "feelables," "clutchables," and "touchables." Beware of bombarding your infant with too many sound and sight experiences. An infant needs quiet to learn and practice. Don't get disturbed if your baby does them over and over again. That's a child's way of adding information to his or her memory bank.

Item	Age in Weeks	Describe Infant Reactions
Baby mirror, wall mirror, or hand mirror		
Hair dryer (warm and cool air)		
Fingering wavy surface of washboard		
Soap bubbles		
Sand or sawdust		
Water play		
Ticking clock and chimes		

RECORD 23 (CONTINUED)

Item	Age in Weeks	Describe Infant Reactions
Phonograph	_____	_____
Music Box	_____	_____
Perfumes	_____	_____
Baby swing	_____	_____
Fur pieces, plush	_____	_____
Being tossed or tickled	_____	_____
Foods with distinctive odors (such as cinnamon)	_____	_____

Other experiences _____

RECORD 24   Recorder _____

Seeing and Reaching Skills
(A Researcher's Record)

EDITOR'S NOTE Infancy researchers emphasize the plasticity of early visual-motor functions. Many believe that increased stimulation can accelerate this development, although several researchers acknowledge that it is still too soon to determine whether there is any long-range significance to increased stimulation. Nonetheless, parents need continuously to match the optimum environment with their baby's emerging abilities. These records are tools to enable you to assess and identify the various abilities of your child, and then to prepare a programed environment for their practice.

Child's Name _____

Behavior	Commonly Observed	Parent's Observations	Dates in Months and Days
Hand regard, followed by swiping at an object	2 mos. 5 days		
Single hand raising	2 mos. 17 days		
Raising both hands	2 mos. 21 days		
Glancing from object to hand and back	2 mos. 27 days		
Eyes on object, hands grasp each other at waistline	3 mos. 3 days		
Glances from object to one hand raised and to other hand at waistline clutching shirt	3 mos. 8 days		

RECORD 24 (CONTINUED)

Behavior	Commonly Observed	Parent's Observations	Dates in Months and Days
Torso moving toward object	3 mos. 15 days		
Both hands to waistline clasped and moving toward object	4 mos. 3 days		
Raising one hand to object, glancing at hand and object	4 mos. 10 days		
Rapid and direct adult-type reach	4 mos. 25 days		
Hand preference emerges; mouths objects	4 to 12 mos.		
Grasps objects with palm and fingers	5 to 9 mos.		
Shakes, hits, drops, throws	6 mos. plus		

RECORD 25   Recorder _____

Patterns of Attachment
(A Researcher's Record)

EDITOR'S NOTE It has been verified that infants as young as eight weeks need a human "mothering" figure with whom to form an attachment. Not only must the person be present and stimulating, the mothering figure must also <u>respond</u> to baby's attachment overtures. This is a two-way, interactive situation. Once an adequate relationship with mother is established, trust in and ties to other humans will quickly follow. Watch your baby and record his progress.

Behavior	Earliest Observation	Commonly Observed	Parent's Observations and Dates
Cries when held by others; stops when held by mother	8 wks.	12 wks.	
Smiles more readily at mother than others	9 wks.	32 wks.	
Scrambles over mother, exploring her person, playing with her face	10 wks.	30 wks.	
Cries when mother leaves	15 wks.	25 wks.	
Attempts by crawling to *follow* when mother leaves the room	17 wks.	25 wks.	
Lifts arms or shouts when sees mother	17 wks.	22 wks.	
When apart from mother, but still able to see her, baby *orients* toward her	18 wks.	36 wks.	

RECORD 25 (CONTINUED)

Behavior	Earliest Observation	Commonly Observed	Parent's Observations and Dates
Vocalizes more readily with mother nearby	20 wks.	28 wks.	
Buries face in mother's lap, shyness, turning head away, crying	22 wks.	30 wks.	
Clings to mother	25 wks.	40 wks.	
Crawls to favorite person	26 wks.	30 wks.	
Fear of strangers (shyness, turning head away or crying)	28 wks.	32 wks.	
Exploration away from mother using her as a security base	28 wks.	33 wks.	
Distress at separation from mother, even if left with another person, e.g., babysitter	38 wks.	48 wks.	
Tongue thrusting in response to mother's demonstration 2 feet away (test every 3 weeks if possible)	at 6 wks. at ____ wks. at ____ wks.	at 9 wks.	

(The response appears, then disappears, reappears)

Other attachment and interaction behavior _____
_____
_____
_____
_____

RECORD 26   Recorder _____   66

Baby Teeth Formation

EDITOR'S NOTE Your child will wind up with a complete set of "baby teeth" (twenty teeth) by the time she is two and a half. When and in what order vary somewhat from baby to baby. For most babies, tooth-cutting is not an acute discomfort. Permanent teeth start to appear at about six years. We have set down the average time that teeth erupt and fall out. Baby teeth normally occur a little earlier or later. If there are any unusual delays, consult your dentist.

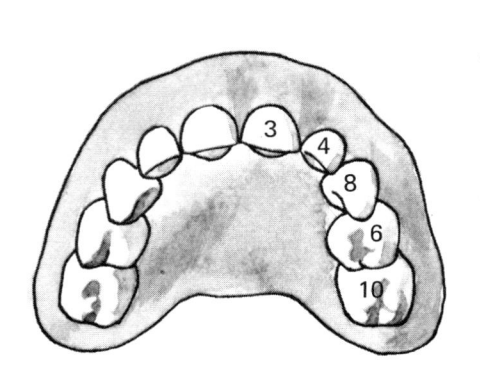

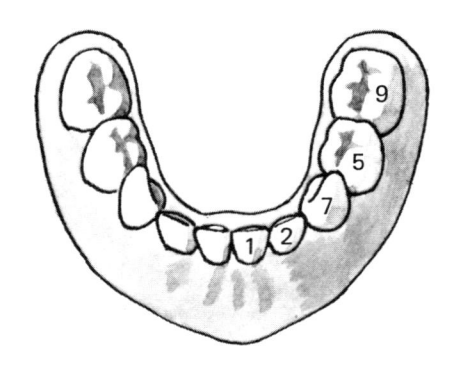

Upper	Average Age Tooth Comes In	Your Child	Average Age Tooth Falls Out	Your Child
3-Central incisor	7½ mos.	_____	7½ yrs.	_____
4-Lateral incisor	9 mos.	_____	8 yrs.	_____
8-Cuspid	18 mos.	_____	11½ yrs.	_____
6-First molar	14 mos.	_____	10½ yrs.	_____
10-Second molar	24 mos.	_____	10½ yrs.	_____
Lower				
9-Second molar	20 mos.	_____	11 yrs.	_____
5-First molar	12 mos.	_____	10 yrs.	_____
7-Cuspid	16 mos.	_____	9½ yrs.	_____
2-Lateral incisor	7 mos.	_____	7 yrs.	_____
1-Central incisor	6 mos.	_____	6 yrs.	_____

There are 20 teeth in the first set, 10 in each jaw.

RECORD 26 (CONTINUED)

Family history of dental problems or missing teeth _____

_____

Describe any tooth-cutting or tooth-formation problems _____

_____

Dentist's recommendations _____

_____

TODDLERS

Second
Twelve
Months
of Life

SECOND TWELVE MONTHS OF LIFE

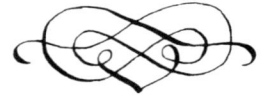

RECORD 27   Recorder _____

Growth and Development–
Twelve to Twenty-four Months

EDITOR'S NOTE The twelfth to twenty-fourth month of life is considered critical by many researchers. The beginning of locomotion (crawling, standing, walking, climbing) spells trouble for parents and caretakers. Socially the child begins to make contact with others outside the family. This is the time when the child is developing personal strategy and style as a social being. Readiness for language and speech is at its prime. (Stimulated disadvantaged children can gain as much as twelve to twenty IQ points in this period.) Ego and self-esteem are built during this time. A knowledge of these vital "ages and stages" is basic to every child caretaker.

Basic Measurements

Weight at 24 months _____   Height at 24 months _____

Shoe size _____   Clothing size _____

Growth and Development (specify date mastered in months)

Body Control

Walks without assistance _____

Uses rocking chair _____

Walks upstairs unaided _____

Runs _____

Jumps _____

Climbs _____

Swings unaided _____

Kicks and throws a ball _____

Pedals kiddie car _____

Language Development

Approximate vocabulary 100-200 words ____

Comprehends "in/out" _____

Comprehends "down/under" _____

Identifies body parts _____

Says own name _____

Identifies 20 pictures _____

Combines noun and verb _____

Small-Muscle Control

Snips with scissors _____

Strings beads _____

Turns pages of book _____

Picks up object without falling _____

Health Habits

Sleeps well _____   fitfully _____

Dresses by himself _____

Puts on _____   takes off _____

_____   _____

Zips and unzips _____

Eats with spoon _____

Cognition

Scribbles on paper _____

Matches like objects _____

Stacks 4 blocks _____

RECORD 27 (CONTINUED)

Favorite records _____

_____

Favorite picture books _____

_____

Child enjoyed _____

_____

_____

Favorite babysitters and caretakers _____

_____

_____

Adaptability to new situations, other people's houses (describe) _____

_____

_____

_____

Play with peers (describe) _____

_____

_____

_____

Second birthday (where and how celebrated) _____

_____

_____

Favorite gifts _____

_____

_____

Memories of the second year of life _____

_____

_____

RECORD 28   Recorder _____   73

Crawling and Creeping

EDITOR'S NOTE To creep the baby must make the four extremities work together. Babies exhibit some amusing antics before they master the skill. To detect developmental phases in this activity, place your baby on her stomach, and watch the way the muscles are then used. As soon as your baby begins to notice toys, move one slowly in order to stimulate the greatest creeping efforts. Continue your observations from birth until your child is able to walk.

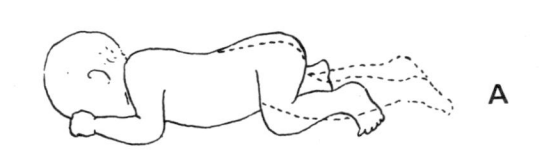

1. The baby holds the legs bent, the knees under the hips, the shoulders and face on the bed, and arms close to the body. Sometimes the head bobs up momentarily and he pushes his legs back and forth as if trying to crawl (A).

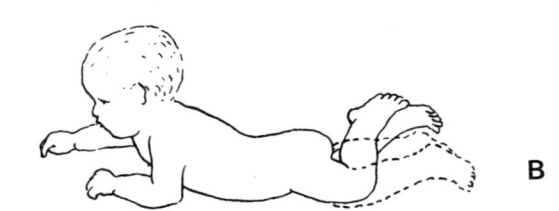

   Onset Date   Comments

   _____   _____
   _____
   _____
   _____
   _____
   _____

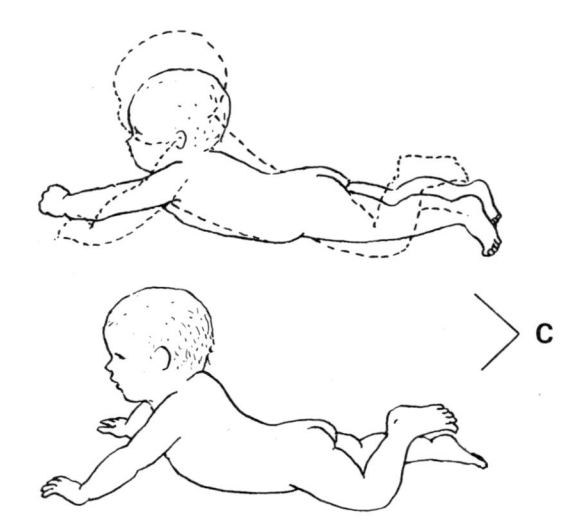

2. The baby is able to hold her head in a lifted position for a few moments; the thighs are less active (B). If the baby is interested, activity increases. She pats the bed, but does not attempt to move her body forward (C).

   Onset Date   Comments

   _____   _____
   _____
   _____
   _____
   _____
   _____

RECORD 28 (CONTINUED)

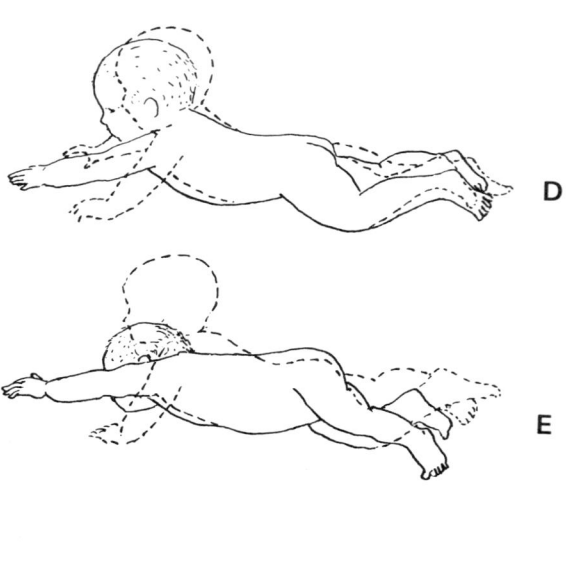

3. The infant keeps his hips flat on the surface as he raises his chest to support himself on his hands. If he tries to reach for an object held before him, his chest goes down, and the wish to move his body is expressed by arm movements (D, E).

Onset Date   Comments

_____   _____
_____
_____
_____
_____
_____
_____

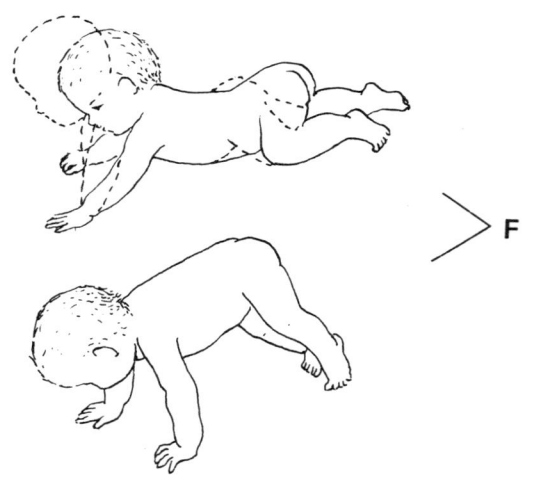

4. She begins to make a distinct effort to move her body forward either by straining to reach or drawing her legs up and pushing. Postural adjustment is not adequate for real creeping. The baby works to gain creeping posture by getting on hands and knees or all fours, but can't maintain the posture and progress. On hands and knees the baby may rock back and forth, but does not make progress (E, F, G).

Onset Date   Comments

_____   _____
_____
_____
_____
_____
_____
_____

RECORD 28 (CONTINUED)

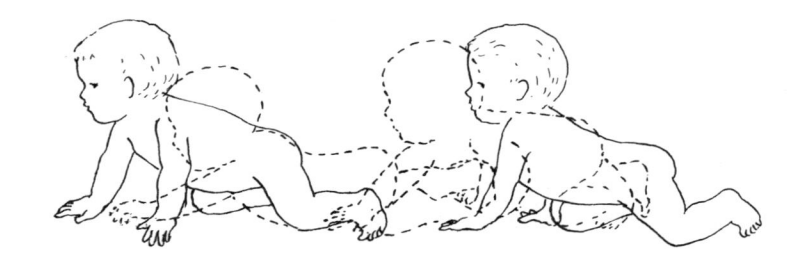

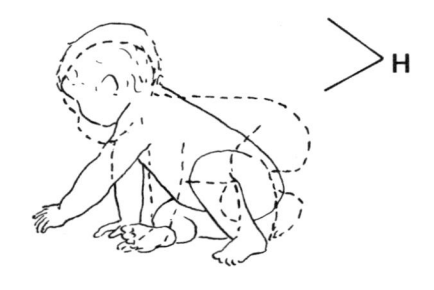

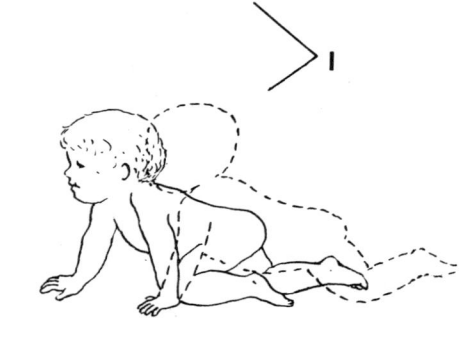

5. The baby can creep about in order to get places, but has no definite method. The movements of arms and legs are quite jerky; he still drops onto his stomach frequently (H).

Onset Date   Comments

_____ _____
_____
_____
_____
_____
_____

6. Finally the infant can creep about lickety-split, utilizing the method of her choice. Whether it is on palms and knees, on all fours, or hitching on her buttocks, she has attained the final stage of this activity. Her movements are well co-ordinated. Also, she creeps in order to get places, not merely to exercise the developing function (I).

Onset Date   Comments

_____ _____
_____
_____
_____
_____
_____

RECORD 29   Recorder _____   76

Standing and Walking*

EDITOR'S NOTE *Three major human skills that must be achieved by an infant during the first three years are (1) standing erect and walking, (2) handling simple tools, and (3) organized speech. Once they are developed, they become tools that enable the child (and adult) to do incredibly complex and inventive things. The manner in which infant and toddler achieve the basic skills reflects fundamental principles involved in the growth process. They cannot be considered as innate or learned; they are a wonderful mixture of both. One easy way to see these connections is to support the baby in an upright position from time to time until the infant gains enough control to stand on her own two feet.*

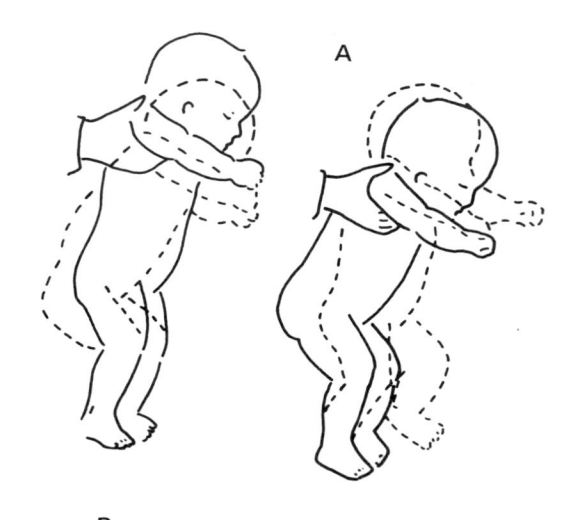

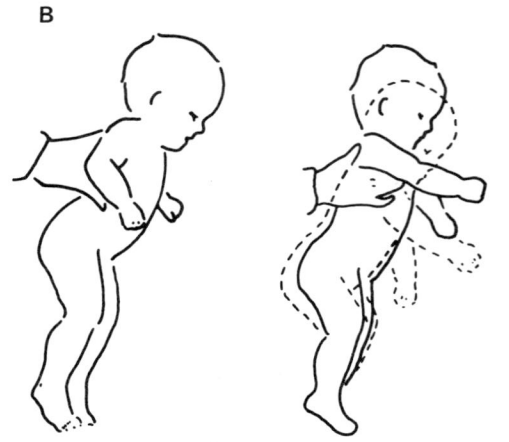

1. When supported under the arms so the feet touch the underlying surface, the baby makes several rhythmical stepping movements—or her legs simply double up beneath her (A).

   Date _____ Yes _____ No† _____

2. The baby stands in a leaning position, the shoulders forward and the head held steadily. The feet are close together, and the baby tends to stand on his toes. You can feel that he is gaining an ability to rest his weight on his own feet. No stepping (B).

   Date _____ Yes _____ No _____

*If you enjoy filling out this record, try filling out other McGraw Records in the Appendix.
†Some stages are skipped by some children. Check *No* where such is the case with your child.

RECORD 29 (CONTINUED)

C D

E

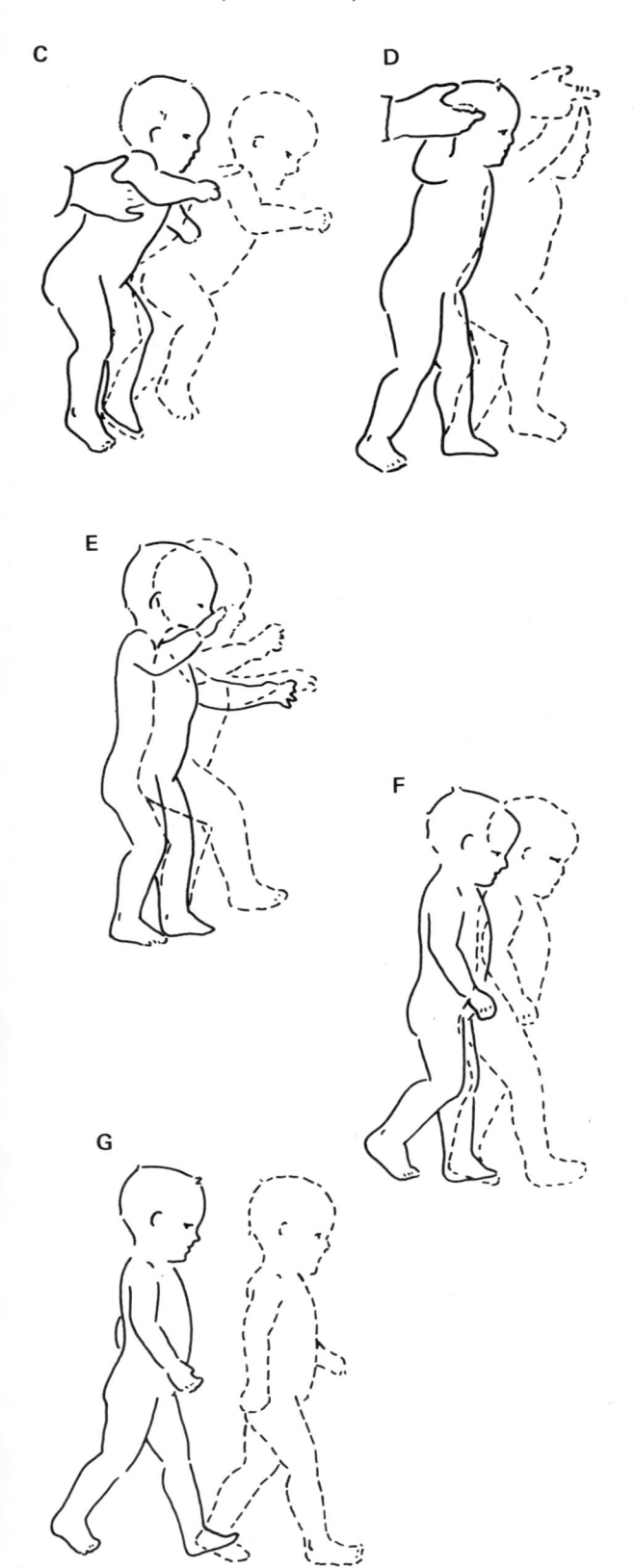

F

G

3. The baby bounces up and down or she stomps, but does not engage in making successive steps. She is beginning to unite the urge to progress with her gain in body support (C).

   Date _____ Yes _____ No _____

4. The baby steps forward with first one and then the other foot when held lightly by the hand. The distance between his feet is wider. His facial expression shows that he is somewhat aware of his steps (D).

   Date _____ Yes _____ No _____

5. The baby begins to walk without help, with arms held out from the body, the feet far apart. The act of walking demands her entire attention; she walks for the sake of walking rather than as a way of getting places (E).

   Date _____ Yes _____ No _____

6. The base becomes less wide, the gait less staggering; the arms are held down by the side of the body, and the child shifts his weight from heel-to-toe as he steps (F).

   Date _____ Yes _____ No _____

7. Finally the child begins to swing her arms rhythmically as she walks and no longer needs to pay attention to the act of walking (G).

   Date _____ Yes _____ No _____

RECORD 30   Recorder _____

Sleep–
Twelve to Twenty-four Months

Behavior	Age	Parents' Observations
Amount of Nighttime Sleep (usually varies from 12 to 15 hrs.)	12-15 mos.	
	16-18 mos.	
	18-21 mos.	
	21-24 mos.	
Daytime Nap (usually 1 to 2½ hrs.)	12-24 mos.	
Sleep Behavior (check appropriate description): ____ Actively resists ____ Consistently takes over 1 hour to fall asleep ____ Wakens during the night ____ Goes to bed willingly (usually) ____ Asleep in 30 minutes (usually) ____ Sleeps through night (usually) or goes back without attention ____ Wakens spontaneously, usually happily ____ Other _____	12-24 mos.	

RECORD 30 (CONTINUED)

Behavior	Age	Parents' Observations
Reasons for Waking:	12-24 mos.	
____ Change of routine		
____ Overtiredness and excitement		
____ Disturbing dreams		
____ Physical discomfort		
____ Other _____		
____ _____		

Sleep Arrangement:	12-24 mos.	
____ Child put to bed same time every night		
____ Sleeps in room alone		
____ Shares room with sibling		
____ Sleeps in parents' room		
____ Other _____		
____ _____		

Describe any unusual sleeptime behaviors (dreams, nightmares, etc.) _____

RECORD 31   Recorder _____

Home Hearing Test at Twelve and Twenty-four Months*

EDITOR'S NOTE To test your child's hearing, begin by having father or an older sibling occupy your child in play or other nonverbal activity while mother moves quietly out of visual range. After the child has been occupied successfully for fifteen to twenty seconds, the mother whispers the child's name and a few simple phrases; for example, "Tom, look at the window!" "Did you see a bird?" "Where is Daddy?" "Tom, raise your hand."—three times from each of three different positions. The mother should whisper three times from the left side of the room, three times from the right side, and three times from middle position (roughly in back of the child), alternating randomly among the three positions for a total of nine whispers.

If your child fails to respond 50 per cent of the time or more, repeat the procedure, but this time the mother should speak in her normal voice instead of in a whisper. Watch your child's face to record responses. There are three possible reactions: (1) No response; (2) Simple alerting: child shows sign of attention by interrupting his activity, raising his head, etc.; (3) Directionally accurate response: child turns toward the direction of the whisper, looks for whispering person, etc.

Examiner _____

	1.	2.	3.	4.	5.	6.	7.	8.	9.
Trials									
Age in Months									
Left Position									
Middle Position									
Right Position									

Parent's comments _____

*Parents should report their "findings" to their child's pediatrician if there is limited response to the regular voice, and even less or no response to the whispered voice. The child may have some hearing problem requiring prompt professional attention.

RECORD 32   Recorder _____

Fears and Dislikes

EDITOR'S NOTE Fear is a normal and healthy feeling that is experienced by all of us at one time or another. Some fears are common ones for growing children. Watch your child's ability to handle fear and provide suitable information and support that will enable her or him to cope.

Fear/Dislike	Age of Onset	How Child Handled it	How Parent Handled it	Age When Terminated
of animals				
of sounds: noises (vacuum cleaner, flushing toilet)				
of people: strangers				
of bodily harm				
of the dark				
of separation, abandonment				
of nightmares				
of new places, situations				
of rejection, loss of love				
others				

PLAY AND
FANTASY

Two to
Four
Years

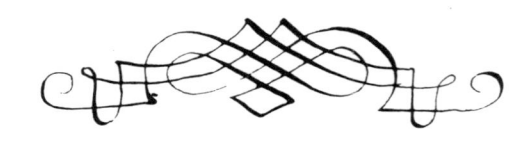

PLAY AND FANTASY
TWO TO FOUR YEARS

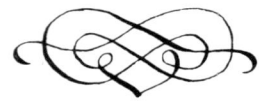

RECORD 33   Recorder _____

Growth and Development–
Two to Four Years

EDITOR'S NOTE This age bracket makes great strides in physical and social maturity, as well as creativity. This is the period of play and fantasy at home or nursery school when self is put aside and toys and peers are shared; when children can learn from reality and play all kinds of situations (community life, family living, hospitals, etc.). Fears, family conflicts, unusual behavior are revealed and are handled by trained parents, nursery school teachers, and therapists. Language takes giant strides because the toddler can listen to stories, hold conversations with peers, and dramatize daily events with well-selected play equipment.

Basic Measurements:

Height at 36 mos. _____   Head size _____   Foot size _____

Weight at 36 mos. _____   Chest circumference _____   Clothing size _____

Growth and Development (specify date mastered in months and days):

Motor Control (Large Muscle)

Walks up stairs unaided _____

Walks on tiptoes _____

Runs _____

Uses rocking horse or chair independently _____
_____

Kicks ball _____

Walks backward _____

Climbs furniture _____

Motor Control (Small Muscle)

Unwraps package _____

Peels a banana _____

Takes objects apart _____

Strings large beads _____

Turns pages one at a time _____

Stacks blocks (5 high) _____

Copies circle on paper _____

Places pegs (medium size) in pegboard _____

RECORD 33 (CONTINUED)

Language Development and Comprehension

Carries out two related commands _____

Uses pronouns "me" and "my" _____

Asks questions: "What's this?" _____

Comprehends "under, over, big, little" _____

Points to and names parts of body on doll
_____

Makes two- or three-word sentences _____

Matches and groups similar objects by color, size, form _____

Counts to 2, aware of one more; knows how many make 2 _____

Names objects that make sounds _____

Self-help and Health Habits

Begins to use fork _____

Asks to go to bathroom _____

Drinks from cup or glass _____

Takes off most of clothing _____

Pours from small pitcher _____

Gets drink without help _____

Socialization

Listens to story and retells simple facts _____

Takes turns in group play _____

Shares play activities _____

Greets visitors _____

Shows affection with dolls, people _____

Shows regard for possessions _____

Initiates own play with simple suggestion
_____

Runs simple errands _____

Other _____

Favorite records _____
_____
_____

Imaginary friends (describe) _____
_____
_____

Playmates (real) _____
_____
_____

Sex identification (wearing pants or dress, interest in bodily parts, prefers playing with boys or girls) _____
_____
_____

Dreaming (describe any problems) _____
_____
_____

RECORD 33 (CONTINUED)

Neighborhood trips your child enjoyed _____
_____
_____
_____
_____

Second birthday (where and how celebrated) _____
_____

Favorite gifts _____
_____
_____

Play at home alone _____ with mother _____
         with peers _____ with father _____
                                            with other children _____

Third birthday (where and how celebrated) _____
_____

Favorite gifts _____
_____

Play at home alone _____ with mother _____
         with peers _____ with father _____
                                            with other children _____

Memories of second and third year _____
_____
_____
_____
_____
_____
_____
_____
_____
_____
_____

RECORD 34   Recorder _____

First Nursery School/Child-care Center

EDITOR'S NOTE *The traditional nursery school emphasizes social skills (interaction with peers) and opportunities to manipulate things and people (ego building). Play is stressed. The Montessori environment emphasizes sensory learning and the practical arts through the use of tangible learning materials. Some preschools are concerned with readiness for reading, writing, and number work.*

In this record we seek information about early adjustments at nursery school or child-care center, and the program offered.

Name of the school _____

Address _____ Telephone _____

Age of your child _____ How long did she go to nursery school? _____

First Day

Did child go willingly to center? _____   Did child join group on arrival? _____

How long did child stay? _____   Did child cling to you? _____

Did you feel guilty about separation? _____

Recall what took place _____
_____
_____
_____

After the first few days, did your child go willingly to the center? _____
_____
_____
_____

RECORD 34 (CONTINUED)

Qualities of a good developmental school or day-care center. A good center should have a cheerful environment with well-trained, loving teachers. Evaluate your center by checking those that describe your child's nursery:

_____ 40-50 ft. of indoor space per child
_____ 100 ft. of outdoor space per child
_____ a nourishing lunch and frequent (nonfattening) snacks
_____ a place to nap, with a cot for each child
_____ available medical attention at center for emergencies or sick child
_____ diapers and changing tables
_____ furniture and toilet facilities adapted to child's height
_____ 2 adults to each group of 8-10 children
_____ ample storage space for each child's clothes
_____ mandatory parent participation

Check Nature of Program

Traditional affective-social emphasis _____ Montessori _____

Preacademic stress _____ Cognitive-discovery approach _____

Other _____

Check Types of Toys and Equipment

_____ Climbing equipment
_____ Hollow blocks (outdoor)
_____ Metal mirror
_____ Rhythm instruments
_____ Large ride'em toys
_____ Autoharp

_____ Woodwork & tools
_____ Good books and records
_____ Puzzles
_____ Parquetry and other design blocks
_____ Children's records
_____ Classical records

Learning Toys
_____ Painting easel
_____ Art supplies: clay, paint, scissors, paper, etc.
_____ Dress-up materials
_____ Giant magnifier
_____ Sand area and sand toys
_____ Trains and cars

Small Toys
_____ Play people
_____ Play animals (farm & zoo)
_____ Family dolls
_____ Design cubes
_____ Family hand puppets
_____ Stringing beads
_____ Montessori materials

Housekeeping Equipment
_____ Play stove, cupboard, etc.
_____ Tea table & chairs
_____ Ironing board & play iron
_____ Doll house & furniture
_____ Doll buggy & cradle
_____ Pots, pans, dishes
_____ Child-sized brooms, mops, etc.

Games
_____ Color matching
_____ Picture lotto
_____ Letter matching

Plants & Animals
_____ Plants
_____ Fish, turtle
_____ Other animals

RECORD 34 (CONTINUED)

Your child's favorite activities _____
_____

Your child's favorite playmates _____
_____

Any special reactions of child _____
_____

Your comments about the value of the school for your child _____
_____
_____
_____

Highlights of teacher's reports _____
_____
_____
_____
_____
_____
_____

(Attach copies of teacher's reports, if available.)

Preschool/Kindergarten Interests and Activities

EDITOR'S NOTE One technique for discovering your child's interests, behaviors, and activities is to observe him on at least two or three occasions a year in a nursery school or play group. Such observations will help you learn in which ways your child is doing well and in which areas some help may be needed. (For example, is your child curious, aggressive, shy, friendly, etc.?) This observation guide is for you and the teacher to fill out while observing. (If you require extra copies of the form, have them Xeroxed at your local library or copy center. Remember to fill one out for each school attended.

Child's Name and Age	Observation Date	Length in Minutes	Observer's Name and Relationship (mother, etc.)
_____	_____	_____	_____
_____	_____	_____	_____
_____	_____	_____	_____

School (1) Check one and list number of years enrolled in school (1), (2), (3)

                 Full day care _____ Full-day preschool _____ Other _____

_____ Five mornings _____ Five afternoons _____ Other _____
Name

School (2) Full day care _____ Full-day preschool _____ Other _____

_____ Five mornings _____ Five afternoons _____ Other _____
Name

School (3) Full day care _____ Full-day preschool _____ Other _____

_____ Five mornings _____ Five afternoons _____ Other _____
Name

RECORD 35 (CONTINUED)

Indicate exact time spent on each different activity.

Minutes Child Spent in Cognitive Activities:
_____ None   _____ Listening to records
_____ Language master   _____ Thinking
_____ Show and tell   _____ Conversing
_____ Typewriter phase   _____ Other _____
_____ Reading corner

Minutes Child Spent on Arts & Crafts:
_____ None   _____ Crayon coloring
_____ Clay   _____ Playdough
_____ Easel painting   _____ Bead stringing
_____ Finger painting   _____ Sewing
_____ Woodworking   _____ Other _____

Minutes Spent in Manipulative Toy Activities:
_____ None   _____ Miniature trucks, trains, etc.
_____ Unit block building   _____ Graduated rings, cylinders; etc.
_____ Large hollow block building _____ Toy animals
_____ Puzzle assembling   _____ Other _____
_____ Doll-house playing

Minutes Spent with Large Motor Activities:
_____ None   _____ Roughhousing
_____ Climbing apparatus   _____ Riding or moving wheeled toys
_____ Pull toys   _____ Swinging
_____ Balancing   _____ Bowling
_____ Running   _____ Other _____

Minutes Spent on Housekeeping:
_____ None   _____ Baby-mothering
_____ Dress-up   _____ Snack Bar
_____ Puppets   _____ Breadwinning figure
_____ Balancing   _____ Being baby
_____ Running   _____ Other _____

Minutes Spent on Scientific Activities:
_____ None   _____ Experiments with chemicals
_____ Water play   _____ Nature
_____ Sand play   _____ Plant observation and care
_____ Animal observation and care _____ Aquarium observation and care
_____ Experiments with physics   _____ Other _____

RECORD 35 (CONTINUED)

Minutes Spent in Kitchen Area:
- _____ None
- _____ Cooking
- _____ Serving
- _____ Eating
- _____ Cleaning
- _____ Other _____

Minutes Spent in Amphitheater Circle Discussion:
- _____ None
- _____ Singing
- _____ Creative drama
- _____ Videotaping a learning episode
- _____ Listening to story
- _____ Telling a story
- _____ Show and tell
- _____ Playing musical instrument
- _____ Free play
- _____ Other _____

Minutes Spent Outdoors:
- _____ None
- _____ Balancing
- _____ Climbing
- _____ Swinging
- _____ Riding wheeled toys
- _____ Sand and/or dirt digging, etc.
- _____ Loading and hauling
- _____ Running
- _____ Sliding and/or rolling down hill
- _____ Other _____

Minutes Spent in Multipurpose Activities:
- _____ None
- _____ Resting
- _____ Sleeping
- _____ Eating
- _____ Seeking isolation
- _____ Quiet games
- _____ Taking group test
- _____ Other _____

Date _____
Teacher _____
Parent _____

RECORD 36   Recorder _____   94

Periodic Preschool Physical Exams— Two to Five Years

(A Professional Record)

EDITOR'S NOTE Schools conduct one or more medical and physical examinations. Ask your school health officer for a copy of such a record. At least one periodic physical examination should be included in this book. The record below was prepared by the National Headstart Office. Xerox several copies for use at various schools. Ask your school doctor to fill one out after each visit. Staple one or more of these to this page.

Name of Child _____ Age _____

Identification of School or Agency _____

Date of This Evaluation _____ Location of This Evaluation _____

_____

A History and Examination was Performed by _____

Date _____ Place _____

Illness, Injuries, Hospitalizations Since Last Evaluation

_____

_____

_____

_____

RECORD 36 (CONTINUED)

Screening Test Since Last Examination

	Not Done	Not Testable	Normal	Abnormal	Remarks
Vision	_____	_____	_____	_____	_____
Hearing	_____	_____	_____	_____	_____
Tuberculin	_____	_____	_____	_____	_____
Anemia	_____	_____	_____	_____	_____
Urinalysis	_____	_____	_____	_____	_____
Other	_____	_____	_____	_____	_____

School Progress _____ Progressing Normal With Age Group _____ Other (Explain) _____

_____

_____

_____

Teachers' Observations

_____ No Apparent Difficulty   _____ Episodic Changes in State of Consciousness, Seizures

_____ Slow or Poor Reader   _____ Hyperactive or Impulsive Behavior

_____ Other (Explain) _____

_____

_____

Changes in Home or Family Setting Since Last Examination
(Moves, New Siblings, Divorce, Unemployment etc.)

_____ None   _____ Other (Explain) _____

_____

_____

Health Problems Noted by Parent or Child

_____

_____

_____

_____

Eye Test—The "E" Game

EDITOR'S NOTE At some period (2½-4 years) you should screen your child's eyes. Some children have better vision in one eye than in the other and often use the stronger eye, with the result that the weaker eye tends to deteriorate. Early detection by parents and doctor can help correct any eye defects before the child enters school.

INSTRUCTIONS FOR PLAYING THE "E" GAME

Play the "E" game at home so that your child will be better prepared for his or her next eye examination by the doctor. Use the large "E" on the next page. When your child is successful with this, write to the National Society for the Prevention of Blindness (79 Madison Ave., New York, N.Y. 10016) for their *free* Preschool Eye Test. It is more extensive than this one.

Directions:
1. Say: "Let's play a game. Do whatever I do. It's like Simple Simon."
2. Extend three fingers of your hand and point them down, up, and toward each side. Repeat until your child can copy you.
3. Hold page in hand so that the prongs of "E" and your fingers point in the same direction.
4. Play the game until the child follows without hesitating.
5. Then only use "E". See if she can point her fingers in the same direction.

| Point Up | Point Down | Point This Way | Point That Way |

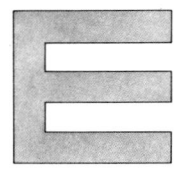

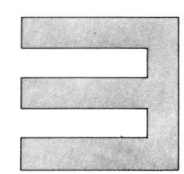

RECORD 37 (CONTINUED)

Eye Test — The "E" Game (see previous page for instructions)

RECORD 38   Recorder _____   98

Visiting the Ophthalmologist

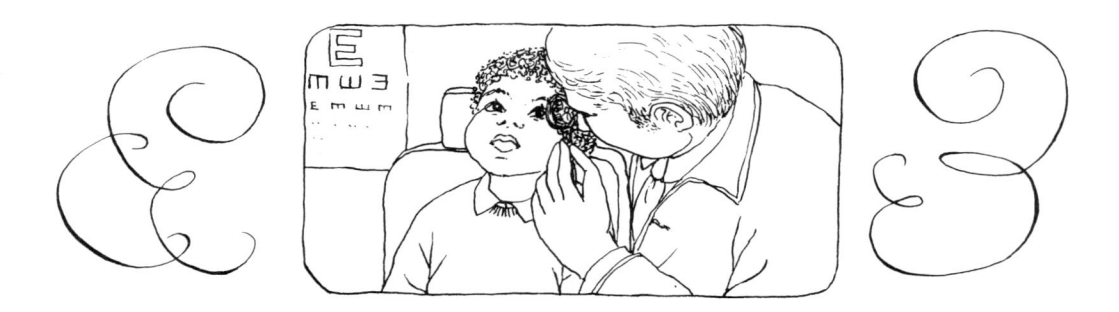

EDITOR'S NOTE *Parents should always get and keep a copy of their child's eyeglass prescription. This makes emergency replacement easier and helps to chart visual changes (for example, from farsighted when younger to nearsighted when older.)*

Dr. _____ Date _____

Address _____
        City   State   Zip

Findings _____

Treatment _____

Progress _____

Eyeglass prescription _____

- -

Dr. _____ Date _____

Address _____
        City   State   Zip

Findings _____

Treatment _____

Progress _____

Eyeglass prescription _____

- -

RECORD 38 (CONTINUED)

Dr. _____ Date _____

Address _____
                                       City   State   Zip

Findings _____

_____

Eyeglass prescription _____

Treatment _____

Progress _____

- -

Dr. _____ Date _____

Address _____
                                       City   State   Zip

Findings _____

_____

Eyeglass prescription _____

Treatment _____

Progress _____

- -

Dr. _____ Date _____

Address _____
                                       City   State   Zip

Findings _____

_____

Eyeglass prescription _____

Treatment _____

Progress _____

- -

THE
LEARNING CHILD

First Three Years

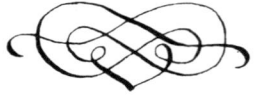

THE LEARNING CHILD
FIRST THREE YEARS

RECORD 39   Recorder _____

Developmental Landmarks in First Three Years

(A Professional Record)

EDITOR'S NOTE Many pediatricians have recommended to parents that they use the Denver Development and Screening Test, approved by the American Academy of Pediatrics, to detect developmental delays. We have reprinted the entire test in the Appendix. Below is a digested version for rapid parental screening. If there are no responses at the approximate age, it may constitute a signal of a possible developmental lag. Discuss it with your doctor.

ABBREVIATED RAPID DEVELOPMENTAL SCREENING TEST

Yes	No	Date	Age	
___	___	_____	1 month	Can he raise his head from the surface while in the prone position?
___	___	_____		Does he regard your face while you are in his direct line of vision?
___	___	_____	2 months	Does she smile and coo?
___	___	_____	3 months	Does he follow a moving object?
___	___	_____		Does he hold his head erect?
___	___	_____	4 months	Will she hold a rattle?
___	___	_____		Does she laugh aloud?
___	___	_____	5 months	Can he reach for and hold objects?
___	___	_____	6 months	Can she turn over?
___	___	_____		Does she turn toward sounds?
___	___	_____		Will she sit with a little support (with one hand)?

RECORD 39 (CONTINUED)

Yes	No	Date	Age	
____	____	_____	7 months	Can he transfer an object from one hand to another?
____	____	_____		Can he sit momentarily without support?
____	____	_____	8 months	Can she sit steadily for about five minutes?
____	____	_____	9 months	Can he say "Ma-ma" or "Da-da"?
____	____	_____	10 months	Can she pull herself up at the side of her crib or playpen?
____	____	_____	11 months	Can he cruise around his playpen or crib or walk holding onto furniture?
____	____	_____	12 months	Can she wave bye-bye?
____	____	_____		Can she walk with one hand held?
____	____	_____		Does she have a two-word vocabulary?
____	____	_____	15 months	Can he walk by himself?
____	____	_____		Can he indicate his wants by pointing and grunting?
____	____	_____	18 months	Can she build a tower of three blocks?
____	____	_____		Does she say six words?
____	____	_____	24 months	Can he run?
____	____	_____		Can he walk up and down stairs holding rail?
____	____	_____		Can he express himself (occasionally) in a two-word sentence?
____	____	_____	2½ years	Can she jump lifting both feet off the ground?
____	____	_____		Can she build a tower of six blocks?
____	____	_____		Can she point to parts of her body on command?
____	____	_____	3 years	Can he follow two commands involving "on," "under," or "behind"?
____	____	_____		Can he build a tower of nine blocks?
____	____	_____		Does he know his first name?
____	____	_____		Can he copy a circle?

RECORD 40   Recorder _____

Language Acquisition During First Three Years
(A Researcher's Record)

EDITOR'S NOTE *Stages of language acquisition are universal, but each baby goes through these stages in his own way, at his own rate. Some psychologists and linguists believe that speech is tied to a child's motor development and unfolds naturally. A few claim that it results from interaction with parents. However, babies who have parents who talk to them seem to talk more. There is need to document this activity with more data from parent observations. Certainly more complex uses of language and communication skills develop through verbal interactions with others.*

Language Activity	Sounds or Words	Date of Onset
1-3 months		
Vocalizes with small throaty noises	_____	_____
Responds to voices and noises	_____	_____
Preverbal communication: cries, laughs	_____	_____
3-6 months		
Coos and laughs aloud: one syllable, vowel-like	_____	_____
Makes loud, high-pitched, squealing sounds	_____	_____
6-9 months		
Babbling, defined as vowels interspersed with consonants: f, v, th and ah-ah-ah and ee-ee-oo	_____	_____

RECORD 40 (CONTINUED)

Sounds made with lips: p, b, m
Consonants made with teeth and gums: t, d, n

9-12 months
Understands "no-no"
Imitates simple syllables: "mama," "dada"
Imitates speech and musical sounds

12-18 months
First words for commands
Labeling: nouns
"Baby talk"

18-24 months
Vocabulary (20-100 words)
Uses nouns and verbs
Sentence length (single-word sentence)
Jargon (stream of gibberish)

24-36 months
Vocabulary (200-900 words)
Uses nouns, verbs, pronouns and adjectives
Sentence length (two-word sentence)

Comments: _____
_____
_____
_____
_____
_____
_____
_____

RECORD 41   Recorder _____

Communication Skills
(A Researcher's Record)

EDITOR'S NOTE Effective communication is a developmental ability, crucial to successful interpersonal relations. It is generally recognized that this ability develops slowly and haphazardly, beginning with the infant's total subjectivity ("the whole world centers on me"), and eventually includes the development of role-taking and empathy (the capacity for participating in another's feelings or ideas).

Age and Stage	Baby-parent and Peer Interactions (include dates of onset)
Newborn-2 yrs. (Subjective, unconscious, sensory-based)	Baby cries, smiles, gestures, vocalizes, talks, uses other modes of communication. Parent responds by _____ _____ _____ Parent picks up, touches, pats, rocks, sings to, scolds, smiles at, talks to baby. Baby responds by _____ _____ _____ _____ Baby initiates less than _____ more than _____ same amount as parent _____
3-8 yrs. (Self and others are fused. Transition stage)	Young child uses words and gestures to express her inner world. Parent responds by _____ _____ _____ _____

RECORD 41 (CONTINUED)

Age and Stage	Child-parent and Peer Interactions (include dates of onset)
	Young child uses words and gestures to express thoughts and feelings to another. Parent responds by _____ _____ _____ _____
	Child initiates less than _____ more than _____ same amount as parent _____
9 yrs. plus (Self and others are separate)	"Middle-aged" child accepts and uses many modes of communication effectively: Speaks with the listener in mind _____ _____ _____ _____
	Listens _____ _____ _____ _____
	Applies meanings _____ _____ _____ _____
	Is able to empathize with other person's feelings _____ _____ _____ _____
	Adjusts vocabulary according to audience _____ _____ _____ _____

RECORD 42   Recorder _____

The Playing Child–Birth to Three Years
(A Researcher's Record)

EDITOR'S NOTE Researchers and psychologists report that early play life has a profound influence on a child's future creativity, drive, self-image, and vocational decisions as well as learning, sensory, and motor development. Your observations will provide invaluable data for assessing your child rearing. (If you wish to share this record with researchers, kindly send photocopies to the Princeton Center for Infancy, 306 Alexander St., Princeton, NJ 08540. We will distribute them to scholars studying the play life of very young children.) Parents will find these records of great interest also.

BODY AND SENSORY PLAY (newborn-6 mo.)

List the beginning week (onset) of the play and most *preferred toy* or *home object*.

Bodily Play

Play with feet _____
                onset (wks.)   favorite foot toy

Sucking _____
                onset (wks.)   object   favorite sucking toy

Fingering _____
                onset (wks.)   object   favorite fingering toy

Sensory Play

Listening _____
                onset (wks.)   object   favorite listening toy

Seeing _____
                onset (wks.)   object   favorite seeing toy

Touching _____
                onset (wks.)   object   favorite touching toy

Grasping _____
                onset (wks.)   object   favorite grasping toy

RECORD 42 (CONTINUED)

Contact Comfort

Describe security objects, toys, blankets, stuffed animals, pillow, doll, clothing _____
_____
_____
_____

Play with Siblings (describe) _____
_____
_____
_____
_____
_____

Verbal Interaction Games with Parent. Describe your child's most active response.

This Little Piggy, Peek-a-boo _____
_____
_____
_____

Imitation of adults _____
_{onset and nature of imitation}
_____
_____

Daily Time Spent	6-12 mos.	12-24 mos.	24-36 mos.	3-6 yrs.
Playing by oneself	_____	_____	_____	_____
With other adults	_____	_____	_____	_____
With other children	_____	_____	_____	_____
With Mother	_____	_____	_____	_____
With Father	_____	_____	_____	_____

MOVEMENT PLAY (6-18 mos.)

List the onset and favorite toys or equipment:

Crawling _____

Standing _____

Pushing and walking _____

RECORD 42 (CONTINUED)

Pull toys _____

Favorite picture books (18-36 mos.) and frequency of use _____
_____
_____
_____

Favorite records and frequency of use _____
_____
_____

Favorite soft toy _____

WALKING AND TALKING (18-36 mos.)

Describe toys and frequency of use. If toys were used for language labeling, vocabulary growth, describe here _____
_____
_____

Toys for balance and walking, riding, etc. _____
_____
_____

Toys for building self-esteem (make your child feel "10 feet tall"), such as puzzles, Color Cone, paint, hollow blocks, kiddie car, ride'em trucks and trains, mirror, etc. _____
_____
_____
_____

RECORD 43   Recorder _____   112

Motor Accomplishments

EDITOR'S NOTE Use this record as a tool to take stock of your baby's progress. Remember that all babies do not develop at the same rate, nor are growth patterns smooth and even. However, children do follow the same sequences of development, and many children even skip one or two stages. Some never crawl, but stand up when they "should be" crawling. This record is concerned with the sequence of motor skills and includes approximate ages at which 50 per cent and 90 percent of large numbers of children achieve them. If your baby is very slow in developing, and this slowness seems to be progressive and increasing, alert your doctor.

Achievement	Age Achieved* (by 50%)	Age Achieved* (by 90%)	Age Achieved by Your Child — Comments
On stomach: chin up, chest up	2 mos.	3½ mos.	_____
On back: turns head freely from side to side	2 mos.	3 mos.	_____
Rolls completely over in any direction	2½ mos.	4½ mos.	_____
Sits with support	3 mos.	4½ mos.	_____
Sits on lap, grasps object	4 mos.	4 mos.	_____

*Do not be concerned whether your baby is in the fiftieth percentile or the nintieth percentile. There is no known advantage to having a "precocious walker." Record the milestones carefully and enjoy your child's progress.

RECORD 43 (CONTINUED)

Achievement	Age Achieved* (by 50%)	Age Achieved* (by 90%)	Age Achieved by Your Child – Comments
Sits in high chair, grasps dangling object	6 mos.	9 mos.	_____
Pre-walking progression: creeping on hands and knees or creeping on hands and feet	7 mos.	11 mos.	_____
Changes from lying to sitting without help	8 mos.	11 mos.	_____
Pulls self up to stand by using furniture	9 mos.	12 mos.	_____
Climbs stair steps	10 mos.	13 mos.	_____
Stands alone	10½ mos.	14 mos.	_____
Walks alone	12 mos.	15 mos.	_____

RECORD 44   Recorder _____   114

Parents' Role in Learning

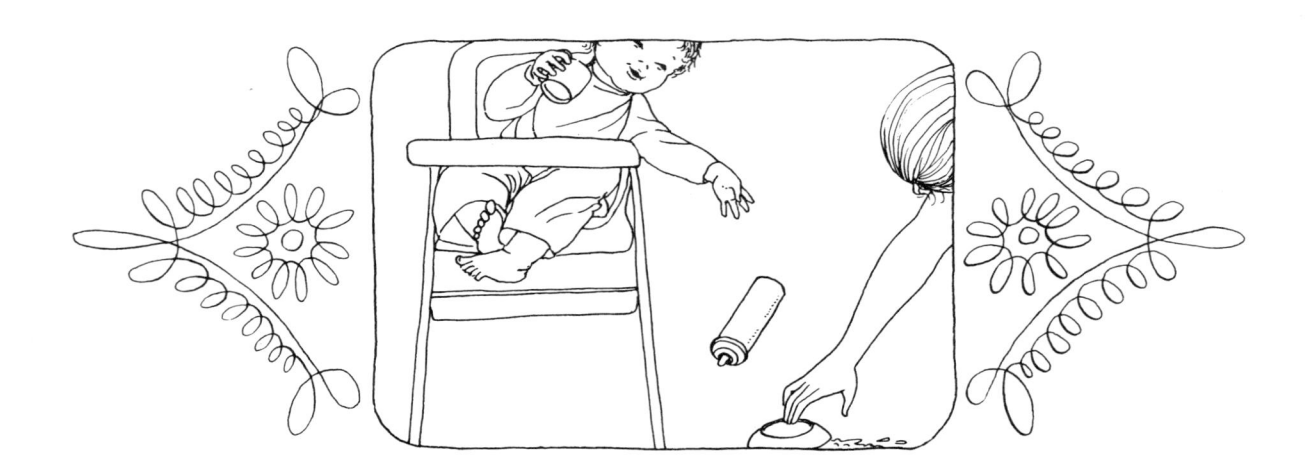

EDITOR'S NOTE Intelligence is greatly influenced by child-rearing practices. For a change, this record is meant for you and not your child. It will help you examine your own behavior as it relates to your baby's growing intelligence. Record dates, comments, and observations. (Read Baby Learning Through Baby Play by Dr. Ira Gordon, St. Martin's Press, and Total Baby Development by Dr. Jaroslav Koch, Wyden Books.)

FROM BIRTH TO ONE YEAR ("the seeds are sown")

Parents provide educational opportunities by changing visual environment

"following games" _____   singing _____
talking _____   other _____

Parent initiates activities, such as

playing with sounds _____ finger-body game _____ mirror _____
parent hides, baby seeks _____
texture games _____ rhythm songs (Pat-a-cake, etc.) _____

Baby initiates, parent expands

Baby vocalizes, parent repeats, imitates _____
Baby drops toys, parent picks them up _____

RECORD 44 (CONTINUED)

Parent empathizes with baby by
Keeping many interesting toys around _____
Changing activities frequently _____

FROM ONE TO TWO YEARS ("the critical period")

Parent provides educational and language opportunities by
Labeling ("This is a ball") _____
Elaborating on child's sentences _____
Relating and explaining ideas _____

Parent initiates activities, such as
Emphasizing consequences ("If you do this, then this happens") _____

_____
_____
_____
_____
_____
_____
_____
_____
_____
_____
_____
_____
_____
_____
_____
_____
_____

THE
CREATIVE YEARS

Four

to Six

Years

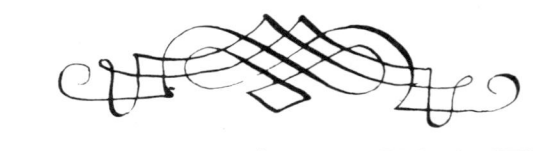

THE CREATIVE YEARS
FOUR TO SIX

Growth and Development— Four to Six Years

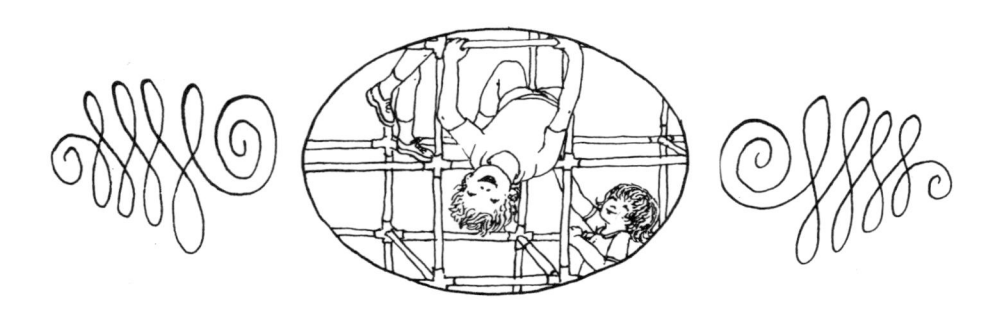

EDITOR'S NOTE Ages four to six are years of great creativity and social growth. Curiosity is at its peak. Each day the child plays out with blocks, play people, and animals, the home events and trips of the preceding days. These experiences become part of the child's language, songs, painting, and basic knowledge. In the preschool and kindergarten, each child finds ample play material and companionship to carry on role-play and fantasy with agemates. Sensitive teachers trained in using play to further social rapport among children know when to let them lead <u>and</u> follow. Learning to live with others enables the child to differentiate right from wrong, and to know the behaviors that will be ignored and those that will be rewarded. These are some of the happiest years of a child's life!

Basic Measurements: at 48 mos.   at 72 mos.   at 48 mos.   at 72 mos.

Height _____ _____	Chest circumference _____ _____
Weight _____ _____	Shoe size _____ _____
Head size _____ _____	Clothing size _____ _____
Waist Circumference _____ _____	

Body Control—Motor Development (specify achievement date in years and months: 4.1, 5.2)

Large Muscle

Climbs, masters playground climbing _____   Masters balance boards _____
Catches and throws beach ball _____   Swings independently _____
Hops on one foot at least 4 steps _____   Bounces large ball _____
Skips _____   Jumps _____   Somersaults without aid _____

RECORD 45 (CONTINUED)

Small Muscle

Copies square or diamond shape _____
Can build pyramids, bridges with blocks in imitation of others _____
Threads long bead chains _____
Uses scissors (blunt-edged) to cut paper ____
Rides a small bicycle _____
Draws a person _____

Understands

Weight (heavy, light) _____
Length (long, short) _____

Self-help and Hygiene

Washes self without help _____
Full bladder control at night _____
Dresses self completely without help _____
Makes imperfect knot _____
Ties a bow _____
Samples new foods _____
Uses spoon and fork efficiently _____
Able to give parents' names, address, phone number _____

Language Development and Comprehension

Knows all body parts _____
Listens to long stories _____
Tells simple events in sequence _____
Counts 4 to 5 objects _____
Counts to 10 _____
Identifies picture differences and likenesses and related objects _____
Names 5 colors _____
Distingusihes coin differences _____
Speaks clearly: vocabulary of 1,500 words ____

Social and Emotional

Separates from mother without crying _____
Seeks child to play with and responds to overtures of another child _____
Plays in group, shares _____
Helps (sets table, cleans up) _____
Shows pride in accomplishments _____
Answers telephone efficiently _____
Makes purchase in store _____
Apologizes _____
Follows directions _____
Persistence (sits 15 minutes to finish task) ____

Sex Identification: describe boy or girl preferences, favorite clothing (dress, pants), bodily contact with father, playing mother role, etc. _____

_____
_____
_____
_____
_____
_____

RECORD 45 (CONTINUED)

Favorite records _____
_____
_____
_____
_____
_____

Birthdays (how celebrated, favorite gifts):

4th Year _____
_____
_____

5th Year _____
_____
_____

6th Year _____
_____
_____
_____
_____

Assists at home (how?) _____
_____
_____

Emotional Problems (sullen, regresses to baby behavior, etc.) _____
_____
_____
_____

Learning Skills (taking lessons)

	How Long	*Where*	*Progress*
Dance (ballet, tap)	_____	_____	_____
Swimming	_____	_____	_____
Piano	_____	_____	_____
Gymnastics	_____	_____	_____
Others	_____	_____	_____
	_____	_____	_____

RECORD 45 (CONTINUED)

Other Achievements

Gets around the community alone. Describe _____

_____

Calls up friends on telephone _____

_____

Goes on overnight sleep-in at friend's house _____

_____

Trips taken (list community trips, other cities, states, countries) _____

RECORD 46   Recorder _____   123

The Playing Child—Four to Eight Years

Group Play

Infant Center _____
               Name   Address

Day-care Center _____

Preschool Center _____

Kindergarten _____

Construction Play (check favorite toys):

_____ Large building blocks	_____ Tinker Toy	Other Construction Toys
_____ Wood puzzles	_____ Meccano	_____
_____ Lego	_____ Erector Set	_____
_____ Bead stringing	_____ Design cubes	_____

Unstructured Play

Home utensils and equipment adapted for play (e.g., pots, keys, chairs, blankets, towels, cardboard boxes): _____
_____
_____

Materials for Exploration (ropes, magnets, prisms, scissors, straws, balloons): _____
_____
_____
_____

Exploring Nature (leaf piles, kites, sand and water, pebbles, shells, growing and planting): _____
_____
_____

RECORD 46 (CONTINUED)   124

Unstructured Construction Play (unit blocks, hollow blocks, color cubes, design toys, collage, finger paints). Describe:_____

_____

_____

_____

Fantasy, Drama, Art & Music Toys (check preferences and underline favorites):

_____ doll-house play	_____ tea table	_____ invention box (bells, buzzers, lights, sockets, etc.)
_____ transportation toys	_____ play people	
_____ playhouse	_____ play store	_____ science toys
_____ painting	_____ clay	_____ dress-up
_____ hand puppets	_____ lotto & matching games	_____ tree house
_____ rhythm instruments	_____ favorite dolls	_____ cut and paste
_____ drawing	_____ child-sized homemaking toys (stove & sink)	_____ metal soldiers
_____ outdoor climbers		_____ mirror (full length)
_____ water and sand play	_____ marionettes & puppets	_____ puzzles

Others:_____

_____

_____

_____

Favorite Play Activity (check):

_____ model building   _____ marionettes   _____ puppetry   _____ dress-up
_____ table games   _____ jokes   _____ riddles   _____ magic

Others:_____

_____

_____

Collecting (check):

_____ playing cards_____ stamps_____ coins_____ comic books_____ butterflies_____ dolls

Others:_____

_____

Competitive Sports

_____ baseball_____ football_____ basketball_____ swimming_____ roller skating

RECORD 46 (CONTINUED)

Others:_____
_____

Play with Peers (check and describe):

_____ aggressive _____ passive _____ dominating _____ leader
_____
_____
_____

Solitary Play (check and describe)

Plays mostly   ____ alone ____ with one child ____ with a group ____ same sex ____ same age
____ opposite sex ____ mixed ____ younger ____ older
_____
_____
_____

Imaginary Playmates. Describe:_____
_____
_____

Parents' Contribution to Play (check)

____ Making doll clothes   ____ Building a tree house   ____ Celebrating holidays
____ Building a doll house   ____ Providing a separate play space ____ Art or music lessons
Others:_____
_____

Vocational Choice (What did she want to be at 5, 10, 15, etc.?)

5-10 yrs. _____
_____

10-15 yrs. _____
_____

15-18 yrs. _____
_____

18-20 yrs. _____
_____

RECORD 47   Recorder _____   126

Social Skills at the Preschool Level

EDITOR'S NOTE *Social competency results from cumulative social activities that your child experiences over a period of years with other agemates. This record of your child's social abilities will be based on your observations of your child in many different situations that pertain to the attributes listed below. (Make duplicate copies of the questionnaire and repeat it at intervals of six months or one year.)*

Age _____   Date _____

How your child relates to other children:
1. Welcomes new members to a group
   ____ verbally
   ____ touches them
   ____ both of the above (or in some other way acknowledges their presence)
   ____ overwhelms them
   ____ ignores them

Other: _____

Example: _____
_____

2. *Your child uses the names of those interacting with her*
   ____ seldom
   ____ usually
   ____ always
   ____ only in small groups

Other: _____

3. *Your child communicates wants by*
   ____ pointing, pulling, crying
   ____ combining action and words
   ____ usually verbalizing
   ____ always verbalizing

Other: _____

Example: _____
_____

RECORD 47 (CONTINUED)

How your child relates to adults
1. When involved in an activity in which help is needed, your child will
____ seek help and information from an adult after an initial independent attempt
____ withdraw from the activity
____ have a temper tantrum (scream, kick, cry)
____ report an accident to any adult
____ attempt to solve the problem; if unsuccessful, will ignore it
____ expect an adult to participate in the activity or at least to be encouraging
Other:_____
Example:_____

2. When adults exercise their authority by setting limits or changing a routine, your child
____ accepts the limits easily   ____ withdraws from the situation or individual
____ is defiant   ____ gets upset

Other:_____
Example:_____

How your child expresses feelings of hostility and pleasure to adults and children
When your child does not get what she wants or when things go just as she wants, your child
____ verbalizes her feelings   ____ withdraws
____ verbalizes her feelings and combines   ____ shares her good feelings with others
    actions with words   and shows pride in her accomplishments
Other:_____
Example:_____

How your child shows leadership
When faced with the prospect of joining a new group, your child
____ enters into the activities in which others are involved
____ initiates activities that are of interest to all the participants
____ takes the lead in shaping the direction of play
____ takes turns or waits to be called on
____ seldom joins the group
____ joins, but frequently interrupts or pushes other
____ usually follows the suggestions of others
Other:_____
Example:_____

RECORD 47 (CONTINUED

How your child behaves in a co-operative venture

1. When your child is involved in a group activity he usually
____ is playful and interacts with the total group
____ is playful and interacts with only one or two others
____ stays alone
____ shares equipment and toys with others willingly
____ does not share equipment and toys easily
____ wanders from activity to activity
____ demonstrates good personal concentration, but is easily distracted by others
____ continues in a task in spite of interruptions
____ stops own play to help another child
____ never helps another child
____ takes turns patiently
____ teases others or pushes ahead

Other: _____

Example: _____

_____

_____

2. Your child's work habits

Does he return property that he has borrowed or does he need to be reminded? _____

_____

Does she ask permission before borrowing something? _____

_____

Does he remember instructions well or does he need to have them repeated? _____

_____

How does she carry out new instructions? Does she forget familiar ones? _____

_____

Does he begin and complete a task promptly? _____

_____

Does she dawdle over assignments? _____

_____

Other: _____

Example: _____

_____

_____

Preschool Personality Development

(FOR PARENT OR TEACHER)
(A Professional Record)

EDITOR'S NOTE This record indicates the many different varieties of behavioral responses that are within the range of expectation. Your child may be short-tempered and extremely curious at the age of five and maintain both of these characteristics as an adult. This record was adapted from System for Open Learning *by John H. Meier, Ph.D., formerly an Associate Professor of Pediatrics, Clinical Psychology, and Education at the University of Colorado Medical Center in Denver. (His three-volume Early Learning Program is one of the best on the market.) Record your observations as objectively as possible. Make a Xerox copy and ask your child's teacher also to fill out a duplicate copy and then compare the two. If you have any serious questions about your child's interests, growth, or behavior, discuss them with the teacher or the doctor.*

Circle the number that best describes your child's behavior at five years

Curiosity:
1 Indifferent or somewhat uninterested in school environment; seems sluggish or depressed.
2 Some tendency to be uninterested in the usual activities; somewhat less alert than peers.
3 Generally alert and exercises initiative in various situations and activities; shows interest and curiosity; rather quick to notice changes in environment; asks questions.
4 Curious and interested in entire environment; explores and tries many new things; asks many questions; initiates conversations and inquiries.

Attention Span:
1 Switches from one toy or activity to another after a relatively short period (less than 5 minutes); attention rather easily drawn away from what he is doing.
2 Medium attention given to each new toy, person, or situation; stays with activities a reasonable length of time (5 to 10 minutes) for child of his age.
3 Continuing interest in most persons, tasks, or things somewhat longer than expected of child at this age (10 to 20 minutes).
4 Continuing interest in same persons, tasks, or things for rather long periods; shows long interest in activities (more than 20 minutes).

Disposition:
1. Any of the following behaviors to an extreme or very noticeable degree: negative, irritable, crying, moody, fussy, hard to get along with, feelings easily hurt.
2. Rarely or seldom irritable or moody.
3. Usually pleasant, co-operative, happy, easy to get along with, good-natured, positive mood.
4. Always very pleasant, co-operative, happy, easy to get along with, good-natured, positive mood.

Activity Level:
1. Usually quiet and inactive; prefers quiet to vigorous play.
2. No preference for active or inactive tasks; not noticeably active or inactive; activity level appropriate for tasks at hand.
3. Noticeably active or quick, but not overactive; prefers active play.
4. Overactive or hyperactive; prefers active tasks and games to inactive ones; movements and amount of activity more than called for by situation; usually or constantly in motion.

Emotional Stability:
1. Little emotional activity; whiny, fretful, or stubborn; depressed or sad; may have temper tantrums or be easily angered; may be out of control; screams and yells at peers and/or adults; hits, bites, kicks, throws and breaks things.
2. Child may show some signs of being fretful, whiny or stubborn, but this behavior is not typical of behavior seen during the day.
3. May have an occasional short period of emotional upset, but is generally even-tempered; quickly regains control.
4. Good emotional stability; even-tempered; absence of temper tantrums, anger, depression; easygoing, relaxed; no real loss of control; smiles and laughs readily.

Interaction with Others:
1. Definite signs of withdrawal; not wanting to be with other children or adults; sucks thumb, fingers, or hair much of the time; shy; ignores activities around him or watches rather than joining in; plays alone most of the time (parallel play).
2. Enjoys being with others, but also enjoys periods for pursuing individual activities; friendly; not noticeably outgoing or withdrawn; plays co-operatively with one or more children.
3. Leans toward outgoingness; co-operative; sensitive to others' rights and feelings.
4. Noticeably outgoing, friendly, affectionate; prefers to play or be with others; very co-operative and sensitive to others' rights and feelings; a leader.

Independence:
1. Demands constant attention and approval; very difficult to separate from mother; wants adults near or to hold him; unusual attachment to one toy, child, or adult.
2. Showing strides toward independence, but reverts to above occasionally.
3. Quite independent; shares ideas; initiates own activities; does not need adults for protection; adjusts easily to new groups and situations; good leader and follower.
4. Rugged individualist; authoritarian leader; independent of all adult and/or child direction or approval; resents intervention of others.

RECORD 48 (CONTINUED)

Parent's or teacher's comments

RECORD 49   Recorder _____

Preschool Health Examination–
Bones and Posture Record
(A Professional Record)

EDITOR'S NOTE To a large extent, posture is inherited, but some postural habits are learned from parents or peer groups. The child with poor posture requires frequent physical examinations to make sure there is no physical abnormality. Once physical disease is ruled out, a formal exercise program supervised by professionals is in order. (Get your doctor to define any medical terminology or condition with which you are not familiar.)

Date _____ Age _____

Birth Information:

Feet and legs: normal _____ pigeon-toed _____

relaxed heel cords _____

twisted shin bone _____

Hips: symmetrical thigh creases _____

range of motion _____

First to Fifth Years:

Feet: flat feet _____ toeing-in _____

Doctor's recommendations: _____

Exercises _____

RECORD 49 (CONTINUED)

Shoe correction _____ Other _____

Posture: slouch _____ round shoulders _____

curvature of spine _____ swayback _____

Thighs: (uneven creases may indicate hip problem) _____
_____

Legs: bowlegs _____ knock-knees _____ abnormal rotation _____

- -

Orthopedic Examination:

Doctor's Name _____

Address _____

Findings _____
_____

Treatment _____ Results _____
_____

Dates visited _____
_____

- -

Orthopedic Examination:

Doctor's Name _____

Address _____

Findings _____
_____

Treatment _____ Results _____
_____

Dates visited _____
_____

- -

Orthopedic Examination:

Doctor's Name _____

Address _____

Findings _____
_____

Treatment _____ Results _____
_____

Dates visited _____
_____

RECORD 50   Recorder _____   134

Preschool or School Dental Health Record

(TO BE FILLED OUT BY DENTIST)
(A Professional Record)

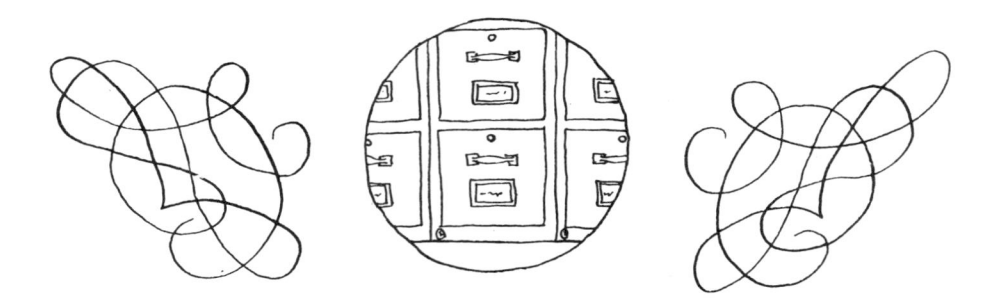

Name of Child _____

Identification of School or Agency _____
Patient's Address _____
Birthplace _____ Sex ____

Has the Child had previous dental care? _____ No _____ Yes

Upper

1 2 3 4 5 6 7 8 | 9 10 11 12 13 14 15 16

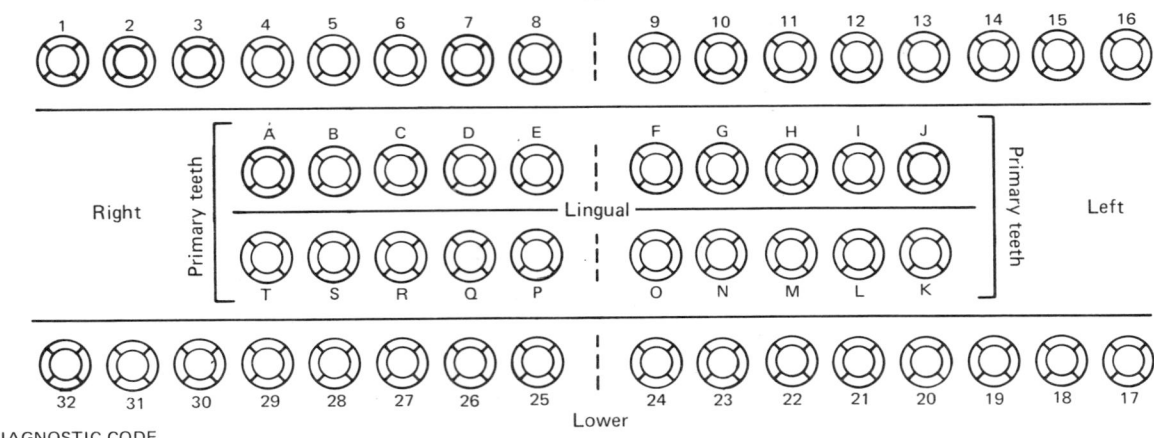

        A B C D E | F G H I J
Right   Primary teeth   Lingual   Primary teeth   Left
        T S R Q P | O N M L K

32 31 30 29 28 27 26 25 | 24 23 22 21 20 19 18 17

Lower

DIAGNOSTIC CODE

- Solid area indicates filling present
- Zebra stripes indicate decay present
- Verticle line indicates to be extracted
- "X" indicates missing tooth

RECORD 50 (CONTINUED)

Services Provided: (please record each treatment on separate line)

Month	Day	Year	Tooth*	Surface*	Material*	Description of Work	Fee	Code	Agency
						Total			

*Treatment Code: Surfaces: M = Mesial, D = Distal, O = Occlusal, L = Lingual, I = Incisal, B = Buccal or Labial
                  Materials: A = Amalgam, S = Silicate, P = Acrylic, C = Steel Crown, O = Other

Important: _____ Check if treatment continued on additional record.

_____ Check if treatment discontinued.

_____ Check if all work for this child has been completed.

Remarks: _____

_____

_____

_____

I hereby certify that the services listed above have been performed

_____

Dentist's signature and address _____

Dentist's License No. _____

RECORD 51   Recorder _____

Care of Permanent Teeth

EDITOR'S NOTE *The first permanent teeth to arrive are the six-year molars. Do not neglect them!*

Permanent Teeth	Date of Eruption	Dental Work Done and Date	Permanent Teeth	Date of Eruption	Dental Work Done and Date
UPPER			LOWER		
Central incisors	_____	_____	Central incisors	_____	_____
Lateral incisors	_____	_____	Lateral incisors	_____	_____
Cuspids	_____	_____	Cuspids	_____	_____
First molars	_____	_____	First molars	_____	_____
Second molars	_____	_____	Second molars	_____	_____

Record of (child's name) _____ *'s Visit to Dentist*

First visit   date _____ Age _____   Fifth visit   date _____ Age _____
Second visit   date _____ Age _____   Sixth visit   date _____ Age _____
Third visit   date _____ Age _____   Seventh visit date _____ Age _____
Fourth visit   date _____ Age _____   Eighth visit   date _____ Age _____

Dental Problems: Check problems and corrections (list others)

Unusual protrusion _____
_____

Incorrect meshing of upper and lower teeth _____
_____

Oral injuries _____
_____

Corrections/treatments (if any) _____

Others _____

Self-image

EDITOR'S NOTE *Self-image is what one thinks of oneself. Sometimes what a person is and what a person thinks of himself are different—for example, the handsome boy who sees himself as ugly or the smart girl who sees herself as dumb.*

List specific examples of your child's

Good Self-image

1 _____
2 _____
3 _____
4 _____
5 _____

Poor Self-image

1 _____
2 _____
3 _____
4 _____
5 _____

1. Is your child's self-image good? _____ poor? _____
2. Explain as best you can, the reasons for the above answer

_____
_____
_____
_____
_____
_____
_____
_____

RECORD 52 (CONTINUED)

_____
_____
_____
_____
_____
_____
_____
_____
_____

Which picture best expresses *your child's attitude* (mark it with an X) when the child is:

with friends _____

at home _____

with brothers and sisters _____

at school _____

with mother _____

with father _____

Which picture best expresses *your child's general attitude* as seen by:

mother _____

father _____

child's friends _____

teacher _____

RECORD 52 (CONTINUED)

Using a scale of 1 through 9, circle one number for each item listed below (1 = the lowest; 5 = the middle; and 9 = the highest).

How would you rate your child's success in developing:

language	1	2	3	4	5	6	7	8	9
speech	1	2	3	4	5	6	7	8	9
listening ability	1	2	3	4	5	6	7	8	9
self-image	1	2	3	4	5	6	7	8	9
perceptual skills	1	2	3	4	5	6	7	8	9
the ability to deal with number concepts	1	2	3	4	5	6	7	8	9
motor development (co-ordination, balance, dexterity, etc.)	1	2	3	4	5	6	7	8	9
telling stories, jokes, riddles, recounting fables, rhymes, poems and pledges	1	2	3	4	5	6	7	8	9

RECORD 53   Recorder _____   141

Attending Kindergarten

_____
Name of School   Address   (public or private)
_____
Teacher   Entrance Age

Full or part-time _____ Distance to school _____ Transportation _____

Nature of curriculum (play, dance, music, creative arts; academics: reading, writing, number work, if any): _____

_____

_____

_____

_____

Child's likes and dislikes in kindergarten: _____

_____

_____

_____

_____

Parent-teacher conferences or report cards (attach) or written reports: _____

_____

_____

_____

_____

Special assemblies or shows: _____

_____

_____

_____

_____

RECORD 54   Recorder _____

Relationship to child _____

Home Behavior Checklist–Ages Four to Six
(TO BE FILLED OUT BY EITHER PARENT OR CARETAKER)
(A Researcher's Record)

EDITOR'S NOTE *Below you will find statements often used by parents to describe children's behavior. Read each statement and decide if it describes your child. If it does, circle T TRUE: if not, circle F FALSE. Example:* 1. Ⓣ F
2. T Ⓕ

It is important to mark *each* statement. If you are in doubt, check the answer which is most correct.

T F 1. Cries easily	T F 13. Afraid of being in cars, or trains, or airplanes, or elevators
T F 2. Whines and complains	T F 14. Wets clothes during the day
T F 3. Shy	T F 15. Nervous habits, such as biting or picking fingernails, twisting hands, rubbing eyes, or pulling hair
T F 4. Dependent; leans heavily on others	
T F 5. Generally considerate and able to share	
T F 6. Finds it hard to talk with others	T F 16. Ambitious: desires to do well and get approval
T F 7. Wets the bed at night at least once a month	T F 17. Poorly co-ordinated when doing things with the hands, such as writing or coloring
T F 8. Constantly fighting or beating up others	
T F 9. Afraid of school; has to be forced to attend	T F 18. Reacts too much to pain, even from slight aches or injuries
T F 10. Frightened of using toilet	
T F 11. Has temper tantrums; yells, screams, cries, kicks feet over the least thing	19. For girls only: Prefers to play with boys
	T F For boys only: Prefers to play with girls
T F 12. Exhibits interest in or concern for others in distress	T F 20. Withdrawn, aloof, unresponsive

RECORD 54 (CONTINUED)

T F 21. Afraid of the dark, thunderstorms, or being alone
T F 22. Fails to carry out tasks at school or home
T F 23. Is clumsy when walking, running, or playing games
T F 24. Generally relaxed and able to concentrate
T F 25. Praises or expresses approval toward adults or other children
T F 26. Good physical co-ordination
T F 27. Responds to simple questions appropriately with "yes" or "no"
T F 28. Takes things in stride; not easily upset
T F 29. Fidgety, some part of body is always moving; can't sit still
T F 30. Engages in artistic activity
T F 31. Thoughts and ideas are sensible and understandable
T F 32. Overtalkative, chatters constantly, interrupts others
T F 33. Refuses to play rough games
T F 34. Picks at food, fusses, or demands special foods
T F 35. Uses the words "today," "yesterday," and "tomorrow" correctly
T F 36. Says or sings a TV commercial, or recites at least one nursery rhyme from memory
T F 37. Talks frequently in sleep
T F 38. Unusually slow at dressing, bathing, eating (dawdles)
T F 39. Is unable to concentrate and meet ordinary requirements of preschool or regular school
T F 40. Exhibits perseverance
T F 41. Enjoys being with children own age

T F 42. Behind in physical development, such as climbing, bike-riding, throwing a ball, etc.
T F 43. Exhausts self; constantly on the go, seldom relaxed
T F 44. Avoids being cuddled or hugged or touched
T F 45. Moves constantly, "gets into everything," swarms all over (overactive)
T F 46. Is as mature as other children own age
T F 47. Gives in to others, does not stand up for self
T F 48. Friendly toward adults
T F 49. Steals at home
T F 50. Shows planning in pursuing an activity
T F 51. Exhibits leadership
T F 52. Recites the alphabet in order
T F 53. Has a good sense of right and wrong
T F 54. Names the days of the week in correct order
T F 55. Does not try new situations, "hangs back" (considered by others as fearful or shy)
T F 56. Smiles and/or laughs frequently
T F 57. Seeks information from adults and children
T F 58. Excessively modest about body, in dressing and undressing, going to the toilet, etc.
T F 59. Communicates verbally with adults and children
T F 60. Secure and confident, seldom worries
T F 61. Bossy with friends
T F 62. Praises self
T F 63. Gets intrinsic satisfaction from an activity or task

RECORD 55 Recorder _____

School Behavior Checklist– Ages Four to Six

(TO BE FILLED OUT BY TEACHER)
(A Professional Record)

EDITOR'S NOTE Below you will find statements often used by teachers to describe children's behavior. Read each statement and decide if it describes the child being rated. If it does, circle T TRUE; if not, circle F FALSE. Example: 1. (T) F
2. T (F)

Note: It is important to mark each statement. If you are in doubt, check the answer which is most often correct.

Child's Name _____ Date _____ Age _____

T F	1. Is friendly
T F	2. Tends to give up if he has something hard to finish
T F	3. Interrupts whoever is speaking
T F	4. Is a helpful child
T F	5. Is alert in class
T F	6. Poorly co-ordinated when doing things with hands, such as coloring or pencil work
T F	7. Just sits around on the playground
T F	8. Acts up when adults are not watching
T F	9. Volunteers to recite in class
T F	10. Hands shake or is nervous when called on to recite

T	F	11. Is considerate of others
T	F	12. Will put up an argument when told not to do something
T	F	13. Teases other children
T	F	14. Is bossy with other children
T	F	15. Is sure of self
T	F	16. Has changeable moods
T	F	17. Gives in when another child insists on doing something another way
T	F	18. Does not respect other people's belongings
T	F	19. Does not forget things which anger her
T	F	20. Seems to be off in own world
T	F	21. Likes an audience all the time
T	F	22. Works well alone
T	F	23. School performance is far below capabilities
T	F	24. Fights back if another child has been asking for it
T	F	25. Is able to concentrate on things
T	F	26. Accepts adult suggestions
T	F	27. Resents even the most gentle criticism of work
T	F	28. Distractible; can't concentrate
T	F	29. Stubborn
T	F	30. Never speaks up, even when there is cause to be angry
T	F	31. Is interested in schoolwork
T	F	32. Never fights back, even if someone hits or pushes first
T	F	33. Prefers to be around adults rather than play with children
T	F	34. Popular with classmates
T	F	35. Never sticks up for self when picked on by other children
T	F	36. Average or above-average IQ (Intelligence Quotient)
T	F	37. Does not take orders when other children are in charge
T	F	38. Prefers to be alone and play alone
T	F	39. Finishes classroom assignments
T	F	40. Slow in making friends
T	F	41. Seems as happy as most children
T	F	42. Seems unconcerned when misbehaving
T	F	43. Is self-confident
T	F	44. When angry, will do such things as slamming the door or banging the desk
T	F	45. Acts in a "daredevil," fearless manner
T	F	46. Has difficulty speaking clearly when excited or upset
T	F	47. Has a "chip on shoulder"
T	F	48. Becomes embarrassed easily
T	F	49. Bright, but doesn't apply self (underachiever)
T	F	50. Disturbs other children with boisterous behavior
T	F	51. Frequent headaches, stomachaches or other nonspecific physical complaints
T	F	52. Plays table games, such as checkers or cards
T	F	53. Recites the alphabet in correct order
T	F	54. Can read words such as "was, letter, deep," etc.

RECORD 56   Recorder _____   146

First-grade Achievements

School _____
          Name   Address

Teacher's Name _____

Tests Given (ask the teacher for copies):

_____
_____
_____

Travel to School (distance from home): _____

walks _____ bicycles _____ buses _____

goes alone _____ accompanied by _____

Favorite Subjects (check 3)

reading _____ number work _____ painting _____

writing _____ show and tell _____ play yard _____

others _____

Parent-teacher Conferences _____

_____
_____
_____
_____
_____
_____
_____
_____

Samples of Printing and Writing:

RECORD 57   Recorder _____   147

Teacher's Health Observations
(TO BE FILLED OUT BY TEACHER)
(A Professional Record)

Identification of School _____

Name of Child _____ Age _____

Name of Teacher _____ Date form Completed _____

Does this child complain of or demonstrate any of the following more severely or more frequently than most of his classmates?

Yes	No		Yes	No	
___	___	Temper Tantrums	___	___	Skin Rash
___	___	Impulsive or Explosive Behavior	___	___	Frequent Scratching
___	___	Hyperactivity or Restlessness	___	___	Sores on Skin
___	___	Withdrawn	___	___	Pale or Sallow Skin
___	___	Inactive or Sluggish	___	___	Continuous Runny Nose
___	___	Sleepy or Lethargic	___	___	Frequent Nose Picking
___	___	Tics or Grimacing			or Rubbing
___	___	Clumsy	___	___	Cough
___	___	Limp or Abnormal Gait	___	___	Wheezing
___	___	Poor Coordination	___	___	Short of Breath with Exercise
___	___	Poor Writing or Drawing	___	___	Overweight
___	___	Convulsions, Fits, or Spells	___	___	Stomachaches
___	___	Spells of Inattention	___	___	Vomiting
___	___	Staring Into Space	___	___	Frequent Urination
___	___	Headaches	___	___	Wets Pants
___	___	Eyes Crossed or Out	___	___	Soils Self with Bowel Movement
___	___	Poor Vision			What is your opinion of this child's health?
___	___	Red, Runny or Itching Eyes	___	___	Perfectly Healthy
___	___	Poor Hearing	___	___	Not in Good Health
___	___	Discharge or Running From Ear	___	___	Specific Problem(s) As Noted
___	___	Unclear Speech			But Generally Healthy

Further observations and explanation of items marked "yes" above

_____
_____
_____
_____

Milestones & Memories

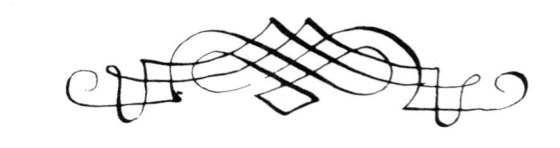

MILESTONES AND MEMORIES

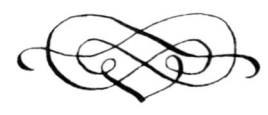

Photo Gallery

EDITOR'S NOTE Select pictures from your photo album that best illustrate the growth of your child from infancy to early adulthood. Lay them out in montage style in the spaces allocated below or have an 8" x 11" photocopy made of the growth and development mural and staple or glue it onto this page.

Newborn

1st year

2nd year

3rd year

4th year

5th year

6th year

8th year

10th year

12th year

14th year

16th year

RECORD 59

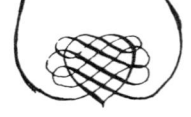

"First Times" in Your Early Life

FIRST HAIRCUT

Before   After

FIRST BIRTHDAY

List date and location:

First train ride _____   First friend _____
First bus ride _____   First job _____
First plane ride _____   First boat ride _____
First movie _____   First _____
First theater _____   _____

RECORD 59 (CONTINUED)

Born on _____, my first day was spent in _____. At home I first slept in a _____. My first toy was given to me by _____. During my first year I followed light with my eyes when I was ____ weeks old. I followed a bell sound at ____ weeks old. I grabbed a rattle when I was ____ weeks old; put rings in my mouth at ____ weeks old. I put my foot in my mouth when I reached age ____. I held a bottle by myself at ____, drank from a cup at ____.

My first educational toy was a _____. I strung beads for the first time when I was age ____; turned pages of a book at ____; named objects at ____. My first soft toy was a _____. My first doll was _____. I had my first tub bath at ____, my first shower on _____. I ate semisolid food for the first time at age ____. I fed myself with my fingers when I was age ____; used a spoon for the first time at ____; a fork at ____; a knife at ____. I washed my face and hands at ____. I pulled my socks off at ____ and shoes at ____; unzipped at ____ and zipped at ____. I crawled for the first time at ____; stood up for the first time at ____; stood by myself at ____; walked at ____; climbed stairs at _____. Toilet learning started at _____; I was completely trained by _____. I pedaled my first kiddie car or tricycle at ____; used a swing independently at ____. I threw a ball at ____; caught my first ball at ____. I did my first somersault at ____. I used scissors at ____.

I laughed for the first time when I was ____; my first word was _____. My first sentence of two words was _____; of five words was _____. I recognized and named three to five pictures in a book when I was ____; named my bodily parts at ____. I could count to three by age ____. My first picturebook was _____. My favorite storybook was _____. I could name five colors when I was ____.

My first games with Mother were _____.
My first games with Father were _____.
My first telephone conversation was with _____. I ate my first ice cream cone when I was ____. The first puzzle I could complete was _____.
                                                                                  (description of puzzle picture)

Additional "firsts" in my early life: _____
_____
_____
_____
_____

RECORD 60   Recorder _____   156

Early Art Efforts

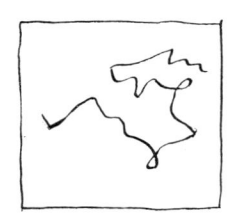

EDITOR'S NOTE As you become familiar with the characteristics of your child's early art attempts, you will be better equipped to respond to and appreciate them for themselves and as part of a developmental process. You will realize that so-called "scribbles" are important and that there are different kinds of scribbles. Try <u>not</u> to label children's pictures and at the same time <u>do not</u> demand labels from them. Replace "Tell me, What is it?" with "Would you like to tell me about your picture?"

THE SCRIBBLE STAGE (2 to 4 years of age)

Characteristics and Use of Materials	*Suggested Materials*	*Observations*
Scribbles at first are disordered, kinesthetic; motions are uncontrolled;	large crayons, smooth, large sheets of paper, poster paints, large brushes	
Characteristics and Use of Materials	*Suggested Materials*	*Observations*
At a more advanced stage, scribbles are more controlled. Strokes are better defined, less diffuse, less repetitive.	newsprint paper, colored construction paper, paste, scissors, clay, felt-tipped pens	
Characteristics and Use of Materials	*Suggested Materials*	*Observations*
At the next level, "naming of scribbles" appears. Strokes are less kinesthetic, more imaginative.	same as above	

RECORD 60 (CONTINUED)

THE PRESCHEMATIC STAGE (4 to 7 years of age)

Characteristics and Use of Materials	Suggested Materials	Observations
The child at this stage discovers the relationship between drawing, thinking, and the environment. Draws a human figure with neck, hands, clothes, and legs.	same as above, plus collage material, needlework, printing, chalk	

THE SCHEMATIC STAGE (7 to 9 years of age)

Characteristics and Use of Materials	Suggested Materials	Observations
The child shows a definite concept of the human figure, of the environment, and of being part of the environment. Pictures include many exaggerations, omissions, and substitutions.	same as above, plus metal, wood	

DAWNING REALISM (9 to 11 years of age—the "Gang" age)

Characteristics and Use of Materials	Suggested Materials	Observations
Attention to clothing of figure Greater stiffness Tendency to realistic lines Emotional approach to color	crayons and colored chalk, metal, clay, wood, collage materials	

Drawing or painting at age ____
(or ceramics, collage, woodwork)

Drawing or painting at age ____
(or ceramics, collage, woodwork)

Drawing or painting at age ____
(or ceramics, collage, woodwork)

Drawing or painting at age ____
(or ceramics, collage, woodwork)

Drawing or painting at age ____
(or ceramics, collage woodwork)

Drawing or painting at age ____
(or ceramics, collage, woodwork)

RECORD 61

Favorite Books

Age Level	Name and Author	Parent's Comments
1 to 2 yrs. Picture book		
2 to 4 yrs. Read aloud		
4 to 8 yrs. Read aloud		
8 to 12 yrs. Reading book		
12 to 14 yrs.		
14 to 16 yrs.		

Your child read alone at age _____
                              Year   Months

First library card obtained _____
                             Year   Months   Library Name and Address

THE
ACADEMIC
YEARS

Six
to
Nine

THE ACADEMIC YEARS
SIX TO NINE

Growth and Development– Six to Nine Years

EDITOR'S NOTE A new world of formal learning opens up to children at this age. Despite the fact that these children are not finished with playing, they recognize that their studies now compete with play needs. They must master reading, number work, writing, spelling, etc. Their movements are restricted by desks and a new code of behavior has to be established. Parents can be sensitive to this conflict and provide at home an environment of play and personal attention to help the child master painlessly the basic academic skills.

Basic Measurements:

	6th Yr.	7th Yr.	8th Yr.		6th Yr.	7th Yr.	8th Yr.
Height	___	___	___	Chest circumference	___	___	___
Weight	___	___	___	Shoe size	___	___	___
Head circumference	___	___	___	Clothing size	___	___	___

Body Maturation (check or describe):

Sports Activities:

swimming _____ skiing _____ roller skating _____

ice skating _____ badminton _____ ping pong _____ bicycling _____

baseball _____ football _____ soccer _____ basketball _____

tennis _____ others(specify) _____

_____

Signs of Puberty (sex organs) _____

_____

RECORD 62 (CONTINUED)

Hobbies (starting age):

constructs models (describe) _____ carpentry _____

collects stamps _____ coins _____ comic books _____ trading cards _____

shells _____ stones/minerals _____ puppetry _____ cooking _____

dolls/doll clothing _____ equipping doll house _____ theater arts (performs in play) _____

other hobbies (specify) _____

Leisure Activities:

Average number of hours spent daily: *Radio*   *Television*   *Movies*   *Books*   *Records*

Comments _____

Favorite TV Programs _____

Favorite Books and Records _____

Clubs and Organizations (at what age) _____

Music Lessons: *Instrument*   *At Age*   *Where*   *Teacher*

RECORD 62 (CONTINUED)

Dancing Lessons: *Kind*   *At Age*   *Where*   *Teacher*

_____   _____   _____   _____
_____   _____   _____   _____

Birthdays (how celebrated):

At 6 Years _____
_____
_____

At 7 Years _____
_____
_____

At 8 Years _____
_____
_____

Academics:

Favorite Academic Subjects _____
_____
_____

Typical Teacher's Evaluation of Progress _____
_____
_____
_____
_____
_____
_____
_____

School Tests and Records

EDITOR'S NOTE A new federal government ruling (Family Educational Rights and Privacy Act of 1974) allows parents to see copies of any intelligence (IQ) aptitude scores, perceptual and academic tests in school, and visual and physical exams. In the early grades, these tests and reports indicate achievements, weaknesses, and efforts of your child. Encouragement and praise can be powerful incentives to personal and academic achievement. Some of these tests are: The Stanford-Binet Intelligence Scales, Wechsler Preschool and Primary Scale of Intelligence, The Slossen Intelligence Test, The Denver Developmental Screening Test, Doll Preschool Attainment Record, The Gates McGennitie Reading Readiness Test, Metropolitan Reading Readiness Test, and various other reading and math achievement tests. Attach copies of school tests and records.

SCHOOL TESTS

Name of Test	Score	Comments

RECORD 63 (CONTINUED)

REPORT CARDS

School & Teacher   *Comments*

1st grade _____
          Teacher's Name

School _____ Address _____

2nd grade _____
          Teacher's Name

School _____ Address _____

3rd grade _____
          Teacher's Name

School _____ Address _____

4th grade _____
          Teacher's Name

School _____ Address _____

5th grade _____
          Teacher's Name

School _____ Address _____

6th grade _____
          Teacher's Name

School _____ Address _____

7th grade _____
          Teacher's Name

School _____ Address _____

8th grade _____
          Teacher's Name

School _____ Address _____

High School

9th grade

School _____

10th grade

School _____

11th grade

School _____

12th grade

School _____

RECORD 63 (CONTINUED)

SPECIAL SCHOOL OR COLLEGE

Undergraduate (school name, dates of attendance)

Dates	Academic Achievements (degrees, honors)	Comments
Freshman year _____	_____	_____
School _____	_____	_____
Sophomore year _____	_____	_____
School _____	_____	_____
Junior year _____	_____	_____
School _____	_____	_____
Senior year _____	_____	_____
School _____	_____	_____

Graduate School (name and dates)	Academic Achievements (degrees, honors)	Comments
_____	_____	_____
_____	_____	_____
_____	_____	_____
_____	_____	_____

Other Information _____
_____
_____
_____
_____
_____
_____
_____
_____
_____
_____

The Emerging Personality

EDITOR'S NOTE *Personality is one of the most difficult qualities to define and record. It has to do with the central core of the child, his unique individuality. It deals with how a child sees himself and how he responds to others. It includes, among other things, fears and fantasies, his personal way of approaching problems, his likes and dislikes, how he handles anger and hostility, and how he learns to postpone gratification.*

Circle the number that best describes your child's coping ability

1	2	3	4	5	6	7
Extremely X	Considerably X	Slightly more X than Y	No more than Y	Slightly more Y than X	Considerably Y	Extremely Y

X							Y
Withdrawn	1	2	3	4	5	6	7	Involved
Masculine	1	2	3	4	5	6	7	Feminine
Tolerates frustration	1	2	3	4	5	6	7	Vulnerable to frustration
Rebellious	1	2	3	4	5	6	7	Compliant
Expressive	1	2	3	4	5	6	7	Restrained
Tense	1	2	3	4	5	6	7	Relaxed
Sensitive to others	1	2	3	4	5	6	7	Self-centered
Submissive	1	2	3	4	5	6	7	Dominant
Active	1	2	3	4	5	6	7	Passive
Apathetic	1	2	3	4	5	6	7	Energetic
Stable	1	2	3	4	5	6	7	Unstable
Solitary	1	2	3	4	5	6	7	Social
Assertive, bold	1	2	3	4	5	6	7	Timid, fearful
Dependent	1	2	3	4	5	6	7	Independent
Constructive	1	2	3	4	5	6	7	Destructive
Aimless	1	2	3	4	5	6	7	Purposeful
Academically motivated	1	2	3	4	5	6	7	Otherwise motivated
Aggressive toward others	1	2	3	4	5	6	7	Affectionate toward others
Socially secure	1	2	3	4	5	6	7	Socially insecure
Rigid	1	2	3	4	5	6	7	Flexible
Happy	1	2	3	4	5	6	7	Unhappy
Shares	1	2	3	4	5	6	7	Possessive
Persists	1	2	3	4	5	6	7	Gives up easily
Active curiosity	1	2	3	4	5	6	7	Lack of interest

RECORD 65

A Record About Me
(TO BE FILLED OUT BY YOUR CHILD)
(You may have to read the questions to him or her)

EDITOR'S NOTE This is a record all about you. There is more to you than you think. You are all the things you like and all the things you don't like, including everything you think and wonder about. To help you think about you, we are asking you to fill out this questionnaire. When you grow older and want to know how you felt about yourself, this record will come in handy.

1. These are important things to know about me.
_____
_____

This is a picture of me in my clothes today.
My clothes are _____ too tight _____ wrinkled _____ just right _____ different from anyone else's

RECORD 65 (CONTINUED)

2. My favorite TV show is _____
   because _____
   _____
   _____
   _____

3. If I were an animal, I would be a _____
   _____
   _____

4. I learn about *me* through my senses (taste, touch, hearing, smelling, seeing)
   I like to smell (check)   My favorite tastes are   I hate these tastes

Yes	No		Yes	No			
___	___	cakes baking	___	___	soap	_____	_____
___	___	zoos	___	___	skunk	_____	_____
___	___	pepper	___	___	after it	_____	_____
___	___	cinnamon			rains	_____	_____
___	___	wood burning	___	___	onions	_____	_____
___	___	perfume	___	___	flowers	_____	_____

5. I like to see (check)
   ____ shapes ____ fuzzy dogs ____ tall buildings ____ other people ____ my house
   ____ sunsets ____ colors ____ my family ____ shadows ____ flowers

6. I like to touch
   ____ sandpaper ____ velvet ____ water ____ fuzzy dogs ____ ice cubes ____ bottles
   ____ erasers ____ fur, and what else? _____ _____ _____ _____
   _____ _____ _____ _____

Today I had lots of feelings
   ____ happy   ____ lazy   ____ peppy   ____ messy   ____ _____
   ____ sad   ____ excited   ____ grumpy   ____ _____
   ____ angry   ____ embarrassed ____ lonely   ____ _____
   ____ sleepy   ____ silly   ____ sick   ____ _____

This is what I keep in my pockets or purse
   ____ gum   ____ a comb   ____ a mirror   ____ _____
   ____ keys   ____ rocks   ____ coins   ____ _____
   ____ a doll ____ string   ____ _____ ____ _____
   ____ a frog ____ buttons ____ _____ ____ _____

When I have a problem
   ____ I let my family solve it   ____ I blame somebody else
   ____ I go outside and play   Also: _____
   ____ I cry   ____ _____
   ____ I think about how to solve it   ____ _____

RECORD 65 (CONTINUED)

My secret places are
a place where I go to be alone _____
a place where I hide special things _____
a place that I just like to think about _____
I hate to be called
    ____ fatso   ____ sissy   ____ skinny   ____ _____ ____ _____
    ____ stupid   ____ honey   ____ scaredy-cat   ____ _____ ____ _____
    ____ stuckup   ____ punk   Also: _____ ____ _____ ____ _____
    ____ kid   ____ buck teeth   ____ _____ ____ _____ ____ _____

I ask questions
    ____ because I don't know the answer
    ____ because I want to learn
    ____ because I already know the answer and
        want everyone to know how smart I am
I would like to know the answer to these questions
_____
_____
_____

The things I worry about most include
_____
_____
_____

The things I fear most are
_____
_____
_____

Sometimes I think or dream about me in other places, in other clothes, doing other things. These are some of my dreams and thoughts _____
_____
_____
_____

Someday I'd like to be
____ a zoo keeper
____ President of the U.S.A.
____ a teacher
____ a musician
____ _____

If I could be anything, I'd want to be
____ an astronomer   ____ a soldier
____ a farmer   ____ a nurse
____ a carpenter   ____ a kid forever
____ a movie star   ____ rich
____ a singer in a rock group   ____ an ice cream taster

People who make me MAD (check)
____ My friends, sometimes
____ My parents
____ My little brother or sister

add others:
____ _____
____ _____
____ _____

RECORD 65 (CONTINUED)

When I am sad I want to
____ hit someone in the nose   ____ go to my room   ____ run away
____ cry   ____ slam a door   ____ plan something really mean
____ _____

Things that make me sad include
_____

My family fusses about
____ what I eat   ____ my friends   ____ my manners   ____ my homework
____ how I act   ____ my hair   ____ my dirty room   ____ _____
____ what I wear   ____ my muddy shoes   ____ my posture   ____ _____
____ my grades   ____ my attitude   ____ my radio   ____ _____

What other people would like me to become

Mother wants me to be
____ an A student
____ a lawyer
____ a dentist
____ _____
____ _____

Father wants me to be
____ a lawyer
____ a football star
____ quiet
____ _____
____ _____

Sister (brother) wants me to be
____ a girl
____ a slave
____ away
____ _____
____ _____

What people think about me
My teacher _____
My _____
My _____

When I am all alone, I think about _____
_____

Things that make me happy _____
_____

I am different than other people in these ways _____
_____

These are things that make me . . . me! _____
_____

ADOLESCENCE

Nine to Sixteen Years

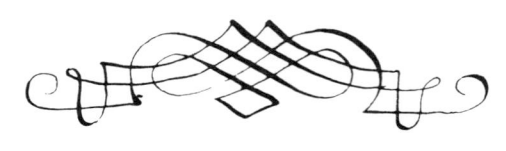

ADOLESCENCE
NINE TO SIXTEEN YEARS

Growth and Development–
Nine to Twelve Years

EDITOR'S NOTE These three years are concerned predominantly with peer relations. This concern shows up in sports, joining of clubs, development of group hobbies, winning awards in swimming, table games, etc. The preteens no longer worry about separation from the family; many welcome sleep-over occasions in the school year as well as summer camps and trips with peer groups. Academically they begin to put together all the unrelated information they have acquired from parents, teachers, television, movies, and peers into a framework of concepts and ideas they will use to understand and evaluate future events.

	9th yr.	10th yr.	11th yr.		9th yr.	10th yr.	11th yr.
Height	_____	_____	_____	Chest circumference	_____	_____	_____
Weight	_____	_____	_____	Shoe size	_____	_____	_____
Head circumference	_____	_____	_____	Clothing size	_____	_____	_____

Peer Groups and Activities (list and describe): _____
_____
_____
_____
_____

Sports (describe favorite ones): _____
_____
_____
_____
_____
_____

Hobbies: _____
_____
_____
_____

RECORD 66 (CONTINUED)

Clubs and Institutions Joined: _____
_____
_____
_____
_____
_____

School and Extracurricular Achievements (participated in school play, sports, and so on):
_____
_____
_____
_____

Academic Achievements:

School attended	_____	Favorite subjects	_____
Grade 4	_____	Grade 4	_____
Grade 5	_____	Grade 5	_____
Grade 6	_____	Grade 6	_____

Typical Teacher Evaluations (list relevant positive and negative reports):
_____
_____
_____
_____

Honor Roll and Other Awards: _____
_____
_____
_____

Social Relations

Favorite Friends At School	In Neighborhood
_____	_____
_____	_____
_____	_____
_____	_____

RECORD 66 (CONTINUED)

Check: Makes friends easily _____ Group leader _____ Follower _____

_____
_____
_____

Photo   Photo   Photo

Describe any guidance or mental health problems requiring professional help

_____
_____
_____
_____
_____
_____
_____
_____
_____

Parents' comments about events, problems in 9th, 10th, 11th years

_____
_____
_____
_____
_____
_____
_____

RECORD 67

Growth and Development—
Twelve to Sixteen Years

EDITOR'S NOTE *At this age all children jump into young adulthood. Bodily, they make great spurts in height and weight; sexually, they become young men and women. They test and practice their sense of independence, to the disturbance of loving parents. Generation gaps develop; parent-child conflicts ensue.*

Basic Measurements	12 yrs.	13 yrs.	14 yrs.	15 yrs.	16 yrs.
Height					
Weight					
Head circumference					
Chest circumference					
Shoe size					
Clothing size					

Body Maturation: Signs of Puberty (menstruation, "wet dreams") _____

_____

_____

_____

_____

Sports Interests (list in order of preference) _____

_____

_____

_____

_____

RECORD 67 (CONTINUED)

Hobbies (list in order of preference) _____
_____
_____
_____
_____

Vocational Interests (describe career interests) _____
_____
_____
_____
_____

Part-time Jobs Held (after school and/or on Saturdays):

12 yrs.	*13 yrs.*	*14 yrs.*	*15 yrs.*	*16 yrs.*
_____	_____	_____	_____	_____
_____	_____	_____	_____	_____

Summer Jobs or Projects:

12 yrs. _____
13 yrs. _____
14 yrs. _____
15 yrs. _____
16 yrs. _____

Leisure-time Favorites:	*12 yrs.*	*13 yrs.*	*14 yrs.*	*15 yrs.*	*16 yrs.*
Books	_____	_____	_____	_____	_____
	_____	_____	_____	_____	_____
TV Programs	_____	_____	_____	_____	_____
	_____	_____	_____	_____	_____
Movies	_____	_____	_____	_____	_____
	_____	_____	_____	_____	_____
Spectator Sports	_____	_____	_____	_____	_____
	_____	_____	_____	_____	_____
Theater Plays	_____	_____	_____	_____	_____
	_____	_____	_____	_____	_____
Other Favorite Activities	_____	_____	_____	_____	_____
	_____	_____	_____	_____	_____

RECORD 67 (CONTINUED)

Social Relations (dating):

First Date _____
            age   with whom (age)   activity

Junior High _____
         (with whom, special events)

_____

_____

High School _____
         (with whom, special events)

_____

_____

Favorite Friends (steady):	12 yrs.	13 yrs.	14 yrs.	15 yrs.	16 yrs.
Boy Friends	_____	_____	_____	_____	_____
	_____	_____	_____	_____	_____
Girl Friends	_____	_____	_____	_____	_____
	_____	_____	_____	_____	_____

Schools Attended:

Intermediate _____
         Name   Address   Principal

Junior High _____
         Name   Address   Principal

High School _____
         Name   Address   Principal

Academic and Sports Achievements:

	12 yrs.	13 yrs.	14 yrs.	15 yrs.	16 yrs.
Report Card	_____	_____	_____	_____	_____
	_____	_____	_____	_____	_____
Favorite Subjects	_____	_____	_____	_____	_____
	_____	_____	_____	_____	_____
Awards	_____	_____	_____	_____	_____
	_____	_____	_____	_____	_____
Elementary Sports	_____	_____	_____	_____	_____
Intermediate Sports	_____	_____	_____	_____	_____
High School Sports	_____	_____	_____	_____	_____

RECORD 67 (CONTINUED)

Teachers' Evaluations (indicate child's age and quote from reports): _____
_____
_____
_____
_____
_____
_____

Favorite Teachers (specify subject taught):

    12th yr.   *13th yr.*
_____   _____
_____   _____

    14th yr.   *15th yr.*
_____   _____
_____   _____

    16th yr.
_____
_____

Comments _____
_____
_____
_____
_____
_____
_____

A "Self" Inventory–Nine to Twelve Years
(A Researcher's Record)

EDITOR'S NOTE It is best for the parent to read each item carefully to a preadolescent child, saying at the start, "This interview is to get you to think about how you really feel about yourself most of the time. Think about the first statements, 'I like the way I look' and 'I hate the way I look.' If you feel that most of the time you like your looks, you should circle 1; if you hate how you look, you should circle 5. If your feeling is somewhere in between, you should circle either the 2, 3, or 4. Try to be as true to your real feelings as possible in all your answers."

Name of child _____ Age of child _____

I like the way I look	1	2	3	4	5	I hate the way I look
I like my name	1	2	3	4	5	I don't like my name

a better name would be _____

I like school	1	2	3	4	5	I don't enjoy school work
I make friends easily	1	2	3	4	5	I am shy and stay by myself
I like being alone	1	2	3	4	5	I like to be with others
I like being me	1	2	3	4	5	I wish I were someone else
I am a pretty stable person and rarely get angry	1	2	3	4	5	I am sensitive and lose my temper easily
I enjoy taking part in group discussions	1	2	3	4	5	I prefer keeping my opinions to myself
My parents love and respect me	1	2	3	4	5	My parents don't love or respect me
My parents understand me	1	2	3	4	5	My parents don't understand me
I do things as well as others my age	1	2	3	4	5	I can't do things as well as others

I generally complete any project I start	1	2	3	4	5	I usually do not complete projects I start
I like being with children my age	1	2	3	4	5	I prefer the company of adults or older children
I like to lead a group	1	2	3	4	5	I would rather be a follower
I am generally happy, peppy, sweet	1	2	3	4	5	More often I am sad, lonely, grumpy
I like being clean, neat	1	2	3	4	5	I like being messy
I am fun to be with	1	2	3	4	5	My friends think I am a grouch
Boys generally like me	1	2	3	4	5	I am not popular with boys
Girls generally like me	1	2	3	4	5	I am not popular with girls
I like to tackle new projects	1	2	3	4	5	I shy away from new projects
I like the way I am built	1	2	3	4	5	I wish my body were built better
I like to read	1	2	3	4	5	I don't enjoy reading
My classmates and I consider myself smart	1	2	3	4	5	I am not as smart as others in my class
I like to do things with my hands	1	2	3	4	5	I don't like to do things with my hands
I am a good manager of my time	1	2	3	4	5	I don't organize my time well
I am a worrier	1	2	3	4	5	I never worry

The Family

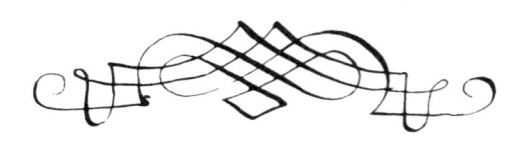

THE FAMILY

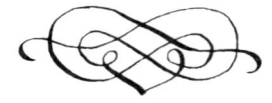

RECORD 69   Recorder _____   191

Father and His Predecessors

(SEE ALSO RECORD 70)

EDITOR'S NOTE *The importance of parents and grandparents to the growing child cannot be overemphasized. Older people provide an anchor, a link to the past. Through intimate association with them, history is lived and fond memories are kept alive. But children also inherit and transmit genetic weaknesses. Be sure to include the following information as it relates to you or your parents. It might be crucial for your child one day. Here and in the following record insert picture if available. List age if living (L) or age at death (D).*

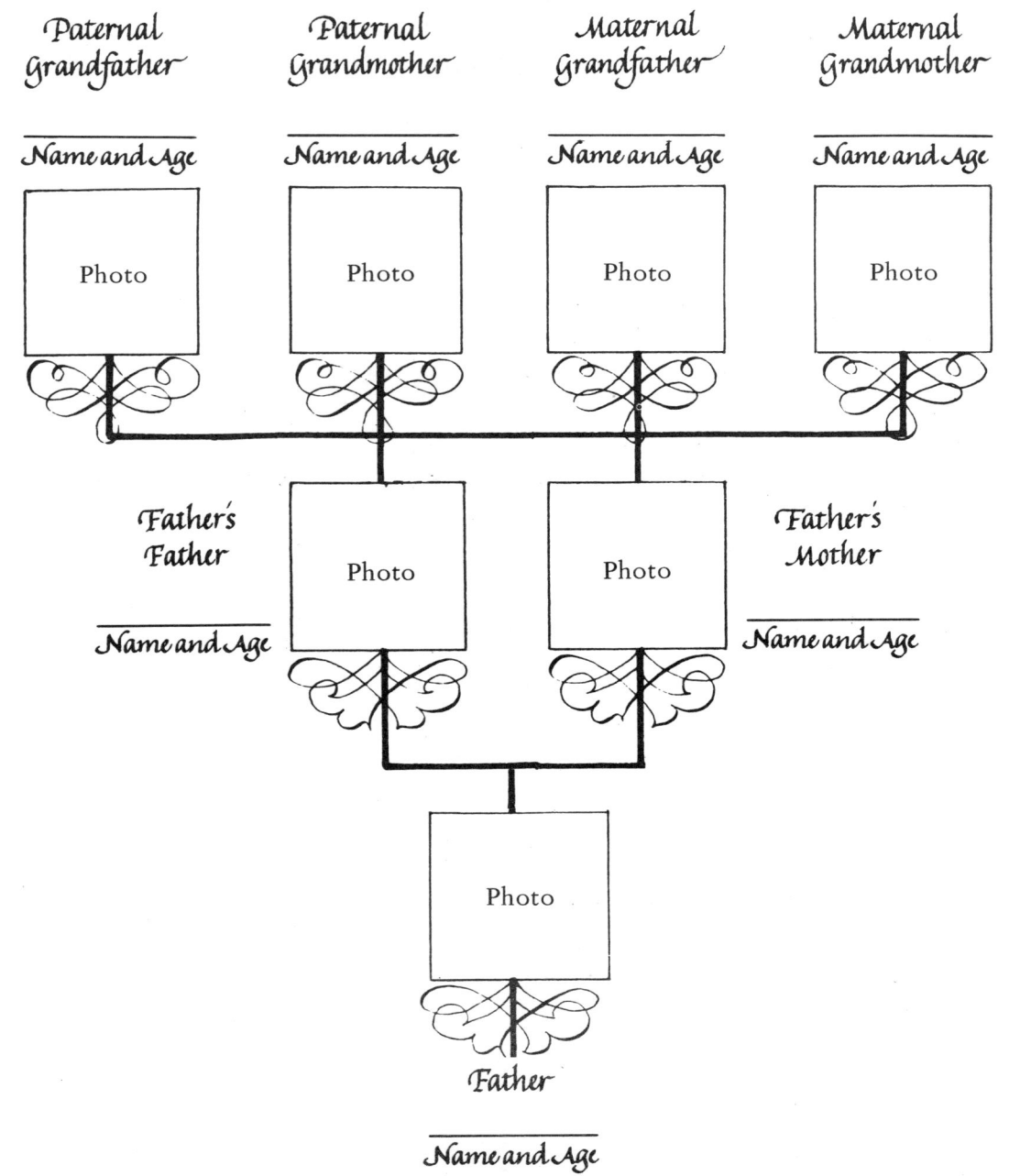

Paternal Grandfather

Name and Age

[Photo]

Paternal Grandmother

Name and Age

[Photo]

Maternal Grandfather

Name and Age

[Photo]

Maternal Grandmother

Name and Age

[Photo]

Father's Father

[Photo]

Name and Age

[Photo]

Father's Mother

Name and Age

[Photo]

Father

Name and Age

RECORD 69 (CONTINUED)

Father's name _____ Age at this recording _____

Father's age when married _____ Birth date and place of birth _____
_____

Father's Adoption if applicable. How old when adopted _____

Where _____ Agency _____

Foster Homes (dates, addresses) _____
_____

Racial Background _____

Father's Marriage Information:

Place of ceremony _____

City _____ State _____

Month _____ Day _____ Year _____ Married by _____

Grandparents' (Father's Parents) Information:

Grandfather's full name _____ Birth date and Place _____

Grandmother's maiden name _____ Birth date and Place _____

Father's guardians (where applicable, include names, dates, and other information)
_____
_____
_____

Father's residences prior to marriage (list city and state) _____
_____
_____
_____
_____
_____
_____

Father's Educational Background (school name and last grade):

Elementary School _____ High School _____

Junior College _____

Post-High School Training (CPA, etc.) _____

4-year College _____ Last Grade or Degree _____

University _____ Graduate Degrees _____
_____

RECORD 69 (CONTINUED)   193

Father's Vocational History:

Father's Social Security No. _____ Present Occupation _____

Prior Occupations _____

_____

_____

_____

Father's Income: _____

Under $5,000 _____ $5,000 to $8,000 _____ $8,000 to $12,000 _____

$12,000 to $20,000 _____ Over $20,000 _____ Over $40,000 _____

Father's Marital Status (when child is 6 years old):

Married _____ Separated _____ Divorced _____ Widower _____

Single Parent _____ Remarried _____ Unmarried _____

Step Parent's Name and Age _____

Father's Medical History:

Allergies _____ Arthritis _____ Cardiac _____ Diabetes _____

Dietary _____ Epilepsy _____ Hearing Defect _____ Obesity _____

Speech _____ Cancer _____ Hypertension _____ Varicose Veins _____

Mental Illness _____

Childhood Illnesses _____

Physical: Weight _____ Height _____ Blood Type _____ Eyes (glasses) _____

Active or Sedentary _____ Condition of teeth _____

Condition of skin _____ Condition of hair _____

Last Medical Checkup: _____
                              Doctor   Institution   Date

If deceased, give age and cause of death _____

_____

Surgery

Hernia _____
            Hospital   Date

Prostate _____
             Hospital   Date

Kidney Stones _____
                  Hospital   Date

Other (specify) _____
                   Hospital   Date

RECORD 69 (CONTINUED)

Father's Siblings (brothers and/or sisters, starting with the oldest):

Name   Sex   *Vital Statistics*   *Schooling*

_____ ___ Birth date _____ died _____ High School: years attended _____
(sibling)
                           Birth place _____ College/Graduate
                                                                        degree   _____
                                                                                Occupation   _____

_____ ___ Birth date _____ died _____ High School: years attended _____
(spouse)
                           Birth place _____ College/Graduate
                                                       degree   _____
                                                       Occupation   _____

Name   Sex   *Vital Statistics*   *Schooling*

_____ ___ Birth date _____ died _____ High School: years attended _____
(sibling)
                           Birth place _____ College/Graduate
                                                       degree   _____
                                                       Occupation   _____

_____ ___ Birth date _____ died _____ High School: years attended _____
(spouse)
                           Birth place _____ College/Graduate
                                                       degree   _____
                                                       Occupation   _____

Name   Sex   *Vital Statistics*   *Schooling*

_____ ___ Birth date _____ died _____ High School: years attended _____
(sibling)
                           Birth place _____ College/Graduate
                                                       degree   _____
                                                      Occupation   _____

_____ ___ Birth date _____ died _____ High School: years attended _____
(spouse)
                           Birth place _____ College/Graduate
                                                       degree   _____
                                                      Occupation   _____

Name   Sex   *Vital Statistics*   *Schooling*

_____ ___ Birth date _____ died _____ High School: years attended _____
(sibling)
                           Birth place _____ College/Graduate
                                                       degree   _____
                                                      Occupation   _____

_____ ___ Birth date _____ died _____ High School: years attended _____
(spouse)
                           Birth place _____ College/Graduate
                                                      degree   _____
                                                      Occupation   _____

RECORD 69 (CONTINUED)

Grandparents' and Great-grandparents' Vital Statistics

Full Names	Date and Place of Birth	Date and Place of Marriage	Last Schooling	Occupation Special Interests
Father's Mother				
Father's Father				
Father's Paternal Grandfather				
Father's Paternal Grandmother				
Father's Maternal Grandfather				
Father's Maternal Grandmother				

Grandparents' and Great-grandparents' Medical History (check)

	Heart	Varicose Veins	Arthritis	Cancer	Diabetes	Hearing Defect	Mental Illness	Age at Death	Cause of Death
Father's Mother									
Father's Father									
Father's Paternal Grandmother									
Father's Paternal Grandfather									
Father's Maternal Grandmother									
Father's Maternal Grandfather									

RECORD 70 Recorder _____ 196

Mother and Her Predecessors

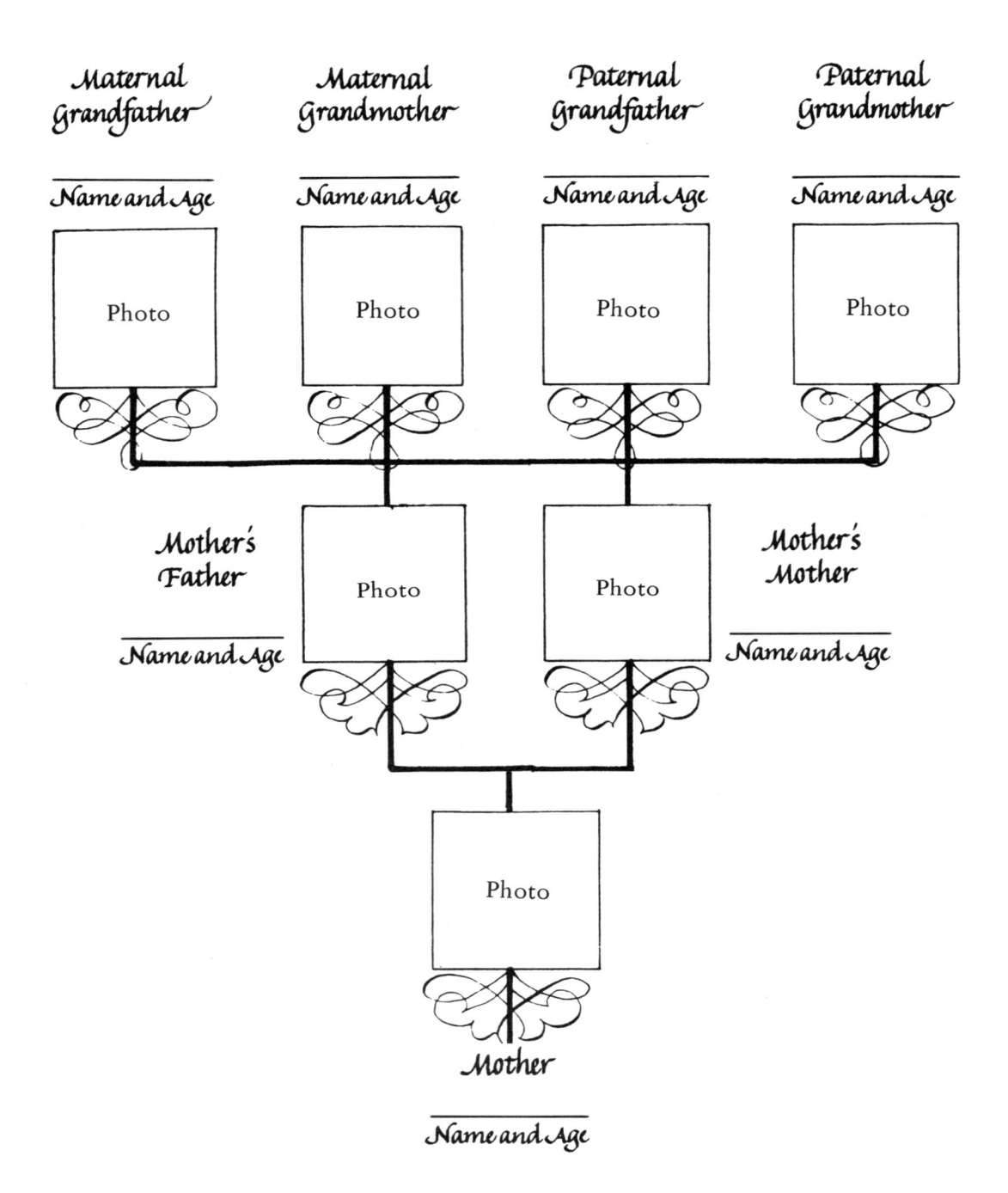

Maternal Grandfather
Name and Age
[Photo]

Maternal Grandmother
Name and Age
[Photo]

Paternal Grandfather
Name and Age
[Photo]

Paternal Grandmother
Name and Age
[Photo]

Mother's Father
[Photo]
Name and Age

[Photo] **Mother's Mother**
Name and Age

[Photo]
Mother
Name and Age

RECORD 70 (CONTINUED)

Mother's Full name _____ Age at this recording _____

Mother's age when married _____ Birthdate and Place of Birth _____

Mother's Adoption if applicable. How old when adopted _____ Where _____ Agency _____

Foster Homes (dates, addresses) _____

_____

_____

Racial Background _____

Maiden name _____

Grandparents' (Mother's Parents) Information:

Grandfather's full name _____ Birthdate and Place _____

Grandmother's maiden name _____ Birthdate and Place _____

Mother's legal guardians (where applicable, include names, dates, and other information):

_____

_____

_____

Residences prior to marriage (list city and state) _____

_____

_____

_____

_____

_____

_____

Mother's Educational Background (school name and last grade):

Elementary School _____ High School _____

Other Post-High School Training (RN, etc.) _____

Jr. College _____ 4-year College _____ Last Grade or Degree _____

University _____ Graduate Degrees _____

Mother's Vocational History:

Mother's Social Security No. _____ Present Occupation _____

Number of hours per week _____

Prior Occupations _____

Mother's Income: _____

Under $5,000 _____ $5,000 to $8,000 _____ $8,000 to $12,000 _____

$12,000 to $20,000 _____ Over $20,000 _____ Over $40,000 _____

RECORD 70 (CONTINUED)

Marital Status (when child is 6 years old):

Married _____ Separated _____ Divorced _____ Widowed _____ Step Parent _____

Single Parent _____ Remarried _____ Unmarried _____

Stepparent's Name and Age _____

Mother's Medical History:

Allergies _____ Arthritis _____ Cardiac _____ Diabetes _____

Dietary _____ Epilepsy _____ Hearing Defect _____ Obesity _____

Speech _____ Cancer _____ Hypertension _____ Varicose Veins _____

Mental Illness _____

Childhood Illnesses _____

Physical: Weight _____ Height _____ Blood Type _____ Rh Factor _____ Condition of Teeth _____

Condition of Hair _____ Condition of skin _____

Eyes (glasses) _____ Active or Sedentary _____

Medical Checkup (last) _____
                       Doctor   Institution   Date

If deceased, give age and cause of death _____

_____

Surgery (mother)

Hysterectomy _____
              Hospital   Date

Gallstones _____
          Hospital   Date

Breast Removed _____
                  Hospital   Date

Other (specify) _____
               Hospital   Date

_____

_____

_____

_____

_____

_____

_____

RECORD 70 (CONTINUED)

Mother's Siblings (brothers and/or sisters, starting with the oldest):

Name   Sex   Vital Statistics   Schooling

_____ __ Birth date ____ died ____ High School: years attended _____
(sibling)   Birth place _____   College/Graduate
                                                   degree   _____
                                                   Occupation   _____

_____ __ Birth date ____ died ____ High School: years attended _____
(spouse)   Birth place _____   College/Graduate
                                                  degree   _____
                                                  Occupation   _____

Name   Sex   Vital Statistics   Schooling

_____ __ Birth date ____ died ____ High School: years attended _____
(sibling)   Birth place _____   College/Graduate
                                                   degree   _____
                                                  Occupation   _____

_____ __ Birth date ____ died ____ High School: years attended _____
(spouse)   Birth place _____   College/Graduate
                                                  degree   _____
                                                  Occupation   _____

Name   Sex   Vital Statistics   Schooling

_____ __ Birth date ____ died ____ High School: years attended _____
(sibling)   Birth place _____   College/Graduate
                                                   degree   _____
                                                  Occupation   _____

_____ __ Birth date ____ died ____ High School: years attended _____
(spouse)   Birth place _____   College/Graduate
                                                  degree   _____
                                                  Occupation   _____

Name   Sex   Vital Statistics   Schooling

_____ __ Birth date ____ died ____ High School: years attended _____
(sibling)   Birth place _____   College/Graduate
                                                   degree   _____
                                                  Occupation   _____

_____ __ Birth date ____ died ____ High School: years attended _____
(spouse)   Birth place _____   College/Graduate
                                                  degree   _____
                                                  Occupation   _____

RECORD 70 (CONTINUED)

Grandparents' and Great-grandparents' Vital Statistics

Full Names	Date and Place of Birth	Date and Place of Marriage	Last Schooling	Occupation/Special Interests
Mother's Mother				
Mother's Father				
Mother's Paternal Grandfather				
Mother's Paternal Grandmother				
Mother's Maternal Grandfather				
Mother's Materna Grandmother				

Grandparents' and Great-grandparents' Medical History (check)

	Heart	Varicose Veins	Arthritis	Cancer	Diabetes	Hearing Defect	Mental Illness	Age at Death	Cause of Death
Mother's mother									
Mother's father									
Mother's Paternal Grandmother									
Mother's Paternal Grandfather									
Mother's Maternal Grandmother									
Mother's Maternal Grandfather									

Fathering

(TO BE FILLED OUT BY BOTH FATHER AND MOTHER)

EDITOR'S NOTE Most children have a hard time recalling what time the father devoted to their upbringing—their care, learning, physical growth, emotional well-being, and their appropriate sex-role identification. Here are some multiple family activities which father and mother can jointly fill out.

Pregnancy and the Newborn:

Father participated with mother in natural and prepared childbirth classes. yes _____ no _____

Father took time off from work to see mother through labor, birth, and homecoming. How much? _____

Attended mother in labor and delivery rooms. yes _____ no _____

Prepared sibling(s), if any, for birth of new baby in family. Describe _____
_____

First 12 Months: Shared in baby care, as indicated below:

10 p.m. & 2 a.m. feedings _____	Soothing crying baby _____
Diaper changing _____	Exercising baby _____
Carriage outings _____	Dressing baby _____
Bathing _____	Bedtime _____
Feeding _____	Shopping for groceries _____
Pla·ing with baby _____	Singing to baby _____

Other _____

Daily Time Spent with Infant: _____ hours

Toddler Period:

Encouraged active exploration of environment _____

Encouraged language by labeling actions and things _____

Fostered independence _____

Took child on trips to park and playground _____

Built child-sized furniture, made toys, etc. _____

Told or read stories at bedtime _____

Helped in toilet learning _____

RECORD 71 (CONTINUED)   202

Went on family camping trips _____
Took toddler to zoo, firehouse, police station _____
Describe other pleasurable, supportive activities _____
_____

Preschool Years (2 to 6):

Cooked with child _____   Took family on vacations _____
Selected playthings _____   Built a tree house _____
Encouraged creative activities (painting, etc.)   Helped organize a co-operative playgroup
_____   _____
Played word and table games _____   Told and read interesting stories _____
Other _____   _____

Some of Father's Outstanding Qualities (check appropriate ones below):

_____ Assertive   _____ Overprotective   _____ Reasonable   _____ Fair
_____ Generous   _____ Understanding   _____ Patient   _____ Loving
_____ Tyrant   _____ Achievement-oriented   _____ Critical   _____ Rough
_____ Demanding   _____ Involved   _____ Protective   _____ Gentle
_____ Cold and aloof   _____ Permissive   _____ Concerned   _____ Sensitive
Other _____

Father as a Model (check below):

_____ He set limits   _____ Taught responsible family behavior
_____ Was a consistent disciplinarian   _____ Furthered a good feeling about the
_____ Acted as an "intellect exerciser"   human body
_____ Taught sex education to his children   _____ Served as a good model of masculine
_____ Helped in child's career choice   behavior

Activities with Father (check below):

_____ Hobbies (stamps, coins, etc.)   _____ Table games   _____ Sports (tennis, baseball,
_____ Sports car rally   _____ Hiking   football, etc.
_____ Backpacking   _____ Fishing   _____ Other_____
Comments _____
_____
_____

The Consistent Caretaker

EDITOR'S NOTE Infant researchers, psychiatrists, and psychologists agree that many emotional insecurities develop early because infants cannot build a feeling of trust and love with one principal caretaker. The age level of 6 to 15 months is especially critical because of fear of strangers and of being abandoned. If a mother returns to work during this period, great care should be taken to provide a steady, loving substitute caretaker—multiple babysitters must be avoided. Who was responsible for the daily care of your child during the following periods?

PRINCIPAL CARETAKER
(mother, father, babysitter, etc.)

Age of Child	Name of Caretaker	Education	Age	What kind of person (loving, gentle, etc.)
0-6 mos.				
6-12 mos.				
12-24 mos.				
2-4 yrs.				
4-8 yrs.				

Mother's absence due to afterbirth illness, surgery, or depression (what and how long) _____

RECORD 72 (CONTINUED)

Father's contribution to caretaking _____
_____
_____
_____

Siblings' contribution to caretaking _____
_____
_____
_____

Relatives' contribution to caretaking (who and how long?) _____
_____
_____
_____

Since birth, has immediate family suffered any major difficulties?

Serious illness _____ Age of Child _____

Death _____ Age of Child _____

Separation _____ Age of Child _____

Divorce _____ Age of Child _____

Remarriage _____ Age of Child _____

Living with relatives _____ Age of Child _____

Other (e.g., moving) _____

Working Mother (List nature of employment, time period):

Age of Child From ___ To ___	*Nature of Employment*	*Full or Part-time*	*Parent's Time Spent with the Child*
_____	_____	_____	_____
_____	_____	_____	_____
_____	_____	_____	_____
_____	_____	_____	_____
_____	_____	_____	_____
_____	_____	_____	_____
_____	_____	_____	_____
_____	_____	_____	_____

RECORD 72 (CONTINUED)

Child-rearing Training

Did either parent have any special training or experience? (Describe any preschool, child development, kindergarten, home economics, pediatric, or nursing training.)

Language spoken in family _____

Size of living quarters _____

Adequate for family? _____

List others living with the family (maid, grandparent, aunt, etc.) _____

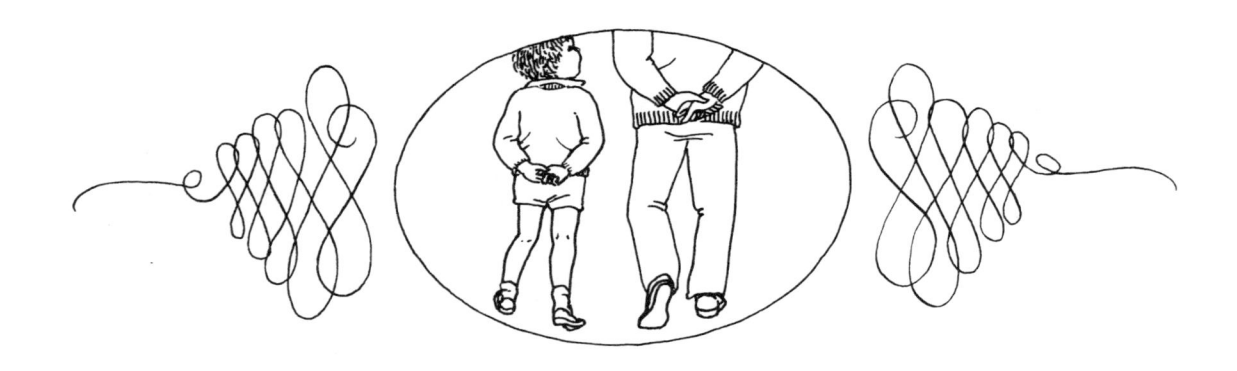

RECORD 73   Recorder _____   206

Brothers and Sisters (Sibling Rivalry)

EDITOR'S NOTE Siblings, older and younger, play an important role in the learning, socialization, self-sufficiency, and creativity of all the children in the family. Describe the co-operation or rivalry that ensued after the birth of the child of this record. Indicate age of child and reaction to younger or older siblings at this recording.

Date at this recording _____ Only Child? _____ Age of Child _____

Brothers and/or Sisters (oldest first) Name and Nickname	Age	Sex	Supportive or Antagonistic

Indicate interactions (rivalry, support, affection, resentment, etc.) of all the children in the family with the child of this record, as well as any interesting close family ties that have continued into adulthood. _____

_____

Describe any strong friendships or relationships outside the family of the child of this record ____

_____

Parents' Attitudes Toward Child Rearing*

EDITOR'S NOTE *Young adults are intrigued with the kind of parenting they had in their early childhood. Were their parents strict, indulgent, permissive? Did they encourage family democracy, sharing, comradeship? Was father considered "the boss" of the family? Did the parents encourage autonomy, independence? Did they approve of rivalry? This questionnaire deals with parents' attitudes on a wide variety of subjects. There are no right or wrong answers, so answer according to your opinion. Since child rearing is not an exact science, you may express your opinion by indicating M(mother) or F(father) in the appropriate column.*

Strongly Agree	Mildly Agree	Mildly Disagree	Strongly Disagree	
_____	_____	_____	_____	Children should be allowed to react to rules their parents make
_____	_____	_____	_____	Shielding a child is very often necessary for her own good
_____	_____	_____	_____	Love is more important than anything else in raising children
_____	_____	_____	_____	A child should be taught to avoid fighting, no matter what happens
_____	_____	_____	_____	A child will be grateful later on for strict training
_____	_____	_____	_____	A young child should be protected from hearing about sex
_____	_____	_____	_____	A wife will not respect a husband unless he assumes the dominant role

*It is important that both mother and father respond.

RECORD 74 (CONTINUED)

Strongly Agree	Mildly Agree	Mildly Disagree	Strongly Disagree	
_____	_____	_____	_____	It is bad for a wife to be so busy and interested in activities outside the home that she does not give her husband the time he deserves
_____	_____	_____	_____	It is natural for children to shy away from a parent who shows a great deal of love and tenderness
_____	_____	_____	_____	A parent should limit the number of hours a child views TV
_____	_____	_____	_____	Parents should ask for their children's opinions and take them into account when something that directly concerns them is decided
_____	_____	_____	_____	Children should consider parents' feelings before they bring into the home snakes and rodents and even domesticated pets
_____	_____	_____	_____	It is better to coax a child into doing something he does not want to do than argue with him
_____	_____	_____	_____	Physical punishment makes a child fear adults and this is the worst thing that can happen to a child
_____	_____	_____	_____	Childhood is too early to expose children to dealing with the problems of death
_____	_____	_____	_____	Parents do not owe children an explanation for their actions
_____	_____	_____	_____	A child should be taught always to come to parents or teachers when he is in trouble rather than to fight
_____	_____	_____	_____	Children should be taught to revere their parents above all other grown-ups
_____	_____	_____	_____	Strict discipline develops a fine, strong character
_____	_____	_____	_____	Too much affection will make a child a "softie"
_____	_____	_____	_____	A child will do better if he learns that showing hurt feelings only makes things worse
_____	_____	_____	_____	It is necessary to let a child experience even unpleasant things
_____	_____	_____	_____	A child has a right to her own point of view and should be allowed to express it

Strongly Agree	Mildly Agree	Mildly Disagree	Strongly Disagree	
_____	_____	_____	_____	A wise parent will teach a child early who is boss
_____	_____	_____	_____	Spanking a child immediately when he is cross and nagging is better than letting him get into the habit of such behavior
_____	_____	_____	_____	What children do not know will not hurt them
_____	_____	_____	_____	Spanking makes it impossible for a child to love and respect her parents
_____	_____	_____	_____	It is good for a child to have lots of attention from relatives
_____	_____	_____	_____	Having to be with the family all the time gives a parent the feeling of having clipped wings
_____	_____	_____	_____	There is no good reason for a child to hit another child
_____	_____	_____	_____	Children who are held to firm rules grow up to be the best adults
_____	_____	_____	_____	A child's pleasure should not come at the cost of a parent's suffering
_____	_____	_____	_____	Most children will test out and even defy rules and regulations before internalizing them
_____	_____	_____	_____	You usually can tell if a child is responsible and competent if he appears to be well-behaved, polite, and deferential
_____	_____	_____	_____	Children who take the initiative are self-starters; they approach new activities and people with enthusiasm, and generally become creative leaders and corporation heads
_____	_____	_____	_____	An only child has a more difficult time growing up than does a child with siblings
_____	_____	_____	_____	Children who are taught by their parents never to be satisfied with what they have done are the ones who get ahead
_____	_____	_____	_____	A child's ideas should be seriously considered in making family decisions
_____	_____	_____	_____	A good parent is a patient parent who is calm, logical, and never yells

RECORD 74 (CONTINUED)

Strongly Agree	Mildly Agree	Mildy Disagree	Strongly Disagree	
_____	_____	_____	_____	There are some things which cannot be settled by a mild discussion
_____	_____	_____	_____	As much as is reasonable, a parent should try to treat a child as equal
_____	_____	_____	_____	A child who is on the go all the time will most likely be happy
_____	_____	_____	_____	If children know parents love them and are always for them, they do what they are told without a fuss
_____	_____	_____	_____	Even in a good marriage a person must sometimes fight for his or her rights
_____	_____	_____	_____	Sex is one of the greatest problems to be contended with
_____	_____	_____	_____	Matter-of-fact treatment of children is better than frequent expressions of feeling
_____	_____	_____	_____	There is no better time than childhood to teach a child to set his goals high
_____	_____	_____	_____	Most wives would do better if they would not appear smarter than their husbands
_____	_____	_____	_____	A child who grows up with the idea that she is going to change everything in the world will end up being a nuisance rather than a help
_____	_____	_____	_____	Children should be kept away from all hard jobs which might be discouraging
_____	_____	_____	_____	It is natural for married people who have minds of their own to quarrel
_____	_____	_____	_____	Most parents prefer a quiet child to a noisy one
_____	_____	_____	_____	Children should at all times be told to fight their own battles
_____	_____	_____	_____	A child is most lovable when he is small and helpless
_____	_____	_____	_____	Children who lie to their parents should be spanked so that they will stop it
_____	_____	_____	_____	A child deserves to be slapped when he talks back to his parents
_____	_____	_____	_____	Children should be taught to work and play hard

RECORD 74 (CONTINUED)

Strongly Agree	Mildly Agree	Mildly Disagree	Strongly Disagree	
_____	_____	_____	_____	Children will be more willing to help and will get more done if they plan their work and do it without the direction of parents
_____	_____	_____	_____	Children should not be encouraged to box or wrestle, because it often leads to trouble or injury
_____	_____	_____	_____	"You have to start early letting them know who's boss; otherwise they'll take advantage and dominate you."
_____	_____	_____	_____	"I like to share my knowledge and experience with my children and then let them make their own decisions."
_____	_____	_____	_____	Conflict is a part of life and not necessarily bad
_____	_____	_____	_____	It's the parents' responsibility to influence their children to do what is best
_____	_____	_____	_____	"I dislike pets, but I tolerate them for my children's sake."
_____	_____	_____	_____	Messy rooms and sloppy outfits are a sure sign that something's amiss
_____	_____	_____	_____	There is something wrong with a child who enjoys playing by himself
_____	_____	_____	_____	The school's function is to teach the three R's. Art, music and moral values fall within the family's province
_____	_____	_____	_____	There is no possible reason for a child to question homework assignments
_____	_____	_____	_____	Children who are given too much leeway and free choice become "hippies"
_____	_____	_____	_____	Brothers and sisters should be treated equally at all times, or sibling rivalry will result
_____	_____	_____	_____	Sending a child to a good preschool and making sure that his or her free time is well spent is a way to guarantee later achievement
_____	_____	_____	_____	It doesn't matter how much carbohydrate you feed babies. There'll be plenty of time for them to diet when they are older
_____	_____	_____	_____	Occasional masturbation is perfectly normal and a temporary, passing phase

Parents' Attitudes Toward Racial and Cultural Differences*

EDITOR'S NOTE No adult would admit that he or she is prejudiced or bigoted. The fact that so many find Archie Bunker so laughable is encouraging. Nevertheless, far too many children grow up with some form of passive or active prejudice based on ignorance, fear, and familial conditioning. This questionnaire will help you identify some of the areas of social interaction in which you might be biased. Express your opinion by indicating M(mother) or F(father) in the appropriate column.

Strongly Agree	*Mildly Agree*	*Mildly Disagree*	*Strongly Disagree*	
_____	_____	_____	_____	Children should be exposed primarily to members of their own race and religion during their earliest years
_____	_____	_____	_____	It's a good idea for your children to attend a nursery school and playground whose population is racially and religiously compatible with your own
_____	_____	_____	_____	It is impossible to teach your child to value and appreciate her own people if cultural diversity also is valued
_____	_____	_____	_____	Children should not be taught the rituals, customs, or songs of other religions

*It is important that both mother and father respond.

Strongly Agree	*Mildly Agree*	*Mildly Disagree*	*Strongly Disagree*	
_____	_____	_____	_____	The motto "Live and let live" is a good one. This line of reasoning applies to all minority groups
_____	_____	_____	_____	It is uncomfortable for children to see slums and human deformities; therefore, children should not be exposed to them
_____	_____	_____	_____	Brotherhood can be taught to children through early exposure to all kinds of cultural groups
_____	_____	_____	_____	Understanding and appreciation of differences foster tolerance, a very desirable human trait
_____	_____	_____	_____	People who associate with people of different racial and religious background are asking for trouble
_____	_____	_____	_____	If my daughter announced that she was adopting a baby of black and white parentage, I would respond affirmatively to her decision
_____	_____	_____	_____	Getting to know someone of a different background through team sports or some other group effort is an excellent way to overcome superficial differences
_____	_____	_____	_____	If a certain group of people in your neighborhood or town is reputed to be undesirable, you'd do well to avoid its members and teach your children to do the same

Parents' Attitudes Toward Their Sex Roles*

EDITOR'S NOTE *This questionnaire deals with your feelings and attitudes about feminine and masculine distinctions. To the degree that you can identify and honestly admit your own feelings, you will be able to accept and love your children. Express your opinion by indicating M(mother) or F(father) in the appropriate column.*

Strongly Agree	Mildly Agree	Mildly Disagree	Strongly Disagree	
_____	_____	_____	_____	Little boys should not be encouraged to play with dolls, to play house, or to dress up in lady's clothes
_____	_____	_____	_____	Little girls should be encouraged to participate in sports, but not to compete or aggressively pursue the traditionally male occupations
_____	_____	_____	_____	Children need a full-time parent in the home in order for them to become well-adjusted adults
_____	_____	_____	_____	It is more acceptable for a boy to use foul language and throw temper tantrums than it is for a girl
_____	_____	_____	_____	Few wives know that husbands are part of the family, too, and as such need some looking after

*It is important that both mother and father respond.

RECORD 76 (CONTINUED)

Strongly Agree	Mildly Agree	Mildly Disagree	Strongly Disagree	
_____	_____	_____	_____	Fathers should be discouraged from showing too much affection to daughters over fourteen years of age
_____	_____	_____	_____	Too many men forget that a father's place is with his family when he is not working
_____	_____	_____	_____	If a woman seeks a job outside the home, her husband should not be expected to assume any of the houshold responsibilities
_____	_____	_____	_____	If a woman is not satisfied at home and wants more in the way of challenge or stimulation, her husband should not stand in her way
_____	_____	_____	_____	The old-fashioned family, where the father was in charge, is best for everyone
_____	_____	_____	_____	Mothers should stay in the home and not return to work until their child is about three years old
_____	_____	_____	_____	Children who know a lot about sex become more curious and are apt to get into trouble
_____	_____	_____	_____	Men appreciate a woman more if she stands up for her own rights and opinions
_____	_____	_____	_____	After giving birth, all women instinctively feel maternalistic toward their newborn
_____	_____	_____	_____	For some married couples, the ideal number of children is none
_____	_____	_____	_____	All things considered, the decision to breast- or bottle-feed is based on a very personal, subjective feeling, and one that should be respected
_____	_____	_____	_____	Giving birth to a child does not necessarily make one the most fit parent for that child
_____	_____	_____	_____	It is better for a child to grow up in a family with two unhappy parents than to have to face life with only one parent
_____	_____	_____	_____	Many new parents feel guilty and upset by the hostility and anger they sometimes feel toward their baby
_____	_____	_____	_____	Parenthood thrusts new responsibilities, both financial and emotional, upon a man—factors that may require rapid adjustment and not a little forbearance

RECORD 76 (CONTINUED)

Strongly Agree	Mildly Agree	Mildly Disagree	Strongly Disagree	
_____	_____	_____	_____	Girls and boys above eight years of age should not be allowed to see each other completely undressed
_____	_____	_____	_____	Most children of both sexes play doctor when they are about four to six years old; this exploratory behavior is both natural and normal
_____	_____	_____	_____	There is usually something wrong with a child who asks a lot of questions about sex
_____	_____	_____	_____	There is no difference between the sexes; therefore, girls should be exposed to and prepared for the same lifetime occupations and recreational pursuits as boys
_____	_____	_____	_____	If your fifth-grader has a sexist teacher, you should have her classroom changed
_____	_____	_____	_____	The traditional nuclear family, consisting of both a mother and a father, is the ideal atmosphere in which to rear a child
_____	_____	_____	_____	The Women's Lib Movement has created a situation in which women and girls are afraid to express their inborn femininity lest they appear old-fashioned or déclassé

RECORD 77

Spiritual and Religious Experiences

EDITOR'S NOTE Describe any active participation of your child in a religious school or center (name and address, when started), favorite religious ceremony, family religious celebrations, choir, dramatics, and other programs. Staple any citations or reports to this page.

Photo

Christmas or Hanukkah and Other Celebrations in Your Child's Early Life

EDITOR'S NOTE Christmas or Hanukkah and other celebrations are an important part of the lives of both parents and children. Set down the outstanding Christmas or Hanukkah in your child's life and describe these occasions.

Age	Where	Who Attended	Rituals	Parents' Comments
1 Yr.	_____	_____	_____	_____
2 Yrs.	_____	_____	_____	_____
3 Yrs.	_____	_____	_____	_____
4 Yrs.	_____	_____	_____	_____
5 Yrs.	_____	_____	_____	_____
6 Yrs.	_____	_____	_____	_____
7 Yrs.	_____	_____	_____	_____
8 Yrs.	_____	_____	_____	_____
9 Yrs.	_____	_____	_____	_____
10 Yrs.	_____	_____	_____	_____
11 Yrs.	_____	_____	_____	_____
12 Yrs.	_____	_____	_____	_____
13 Yrs.	_____	_____	_____	_____
14 Yrs.	_____	_____	_____	_____
15 Yrs.	_____	_____	_____	_____
16 Yrs.	_____	_____	_____	_____

RECORD 78 (CONTINUED)

Use this space for jotting down memories of other special holidays

RECORD 79   Recorder _____

Record of Family Residences

EDITOR'S NOTE Your child will be presented at some time in the future with a request for past residences. A job application, especially for government work, may require this information. Or it may be that he would like to revisit these places with his own child.

Date of Purchase or Rental (from to)	Street Address City, State	Adjustments made Your reasons for move Other comments:
_____	_____	_____
_____	_____	_____
_____	_____	_____
_____	_____	_____
_____	_____	_____
_____	_____	_____
_____	_____	_____
_____	_____	_____
_____	_____	_____
_____	_____	_____
_____	_____	_____
_____	_____	_____
_____	_____	_____
_____	_____	_____

Photo

Family Pets

Age	Animal and Name	Comments
1 Yr.		
2 Yrs.		
3 Yrs.		
4 Yrs.		
5 Yrs.		
6 Yrs.		
7 Yrs.		
8 Yrs.		
9 Yrs.		
10 Yrs.		
11 Yrs.		
12 Yrs.		

Photo

Vacations with the Family

	Date		
Age	(from-to)	Where	What Happened, Others in Party, Events You Enjoyed

Parents' comments _____

Vacations away from the Family
(WITH RELATIVES, FRIENDS, AT CAMP)

Age	Date (from-to)	Where	What Happened, Others in Party, Events You Enjoyed

Parents' comments _____

RECORD 83   Recorder _____

Parents' Reminiscences

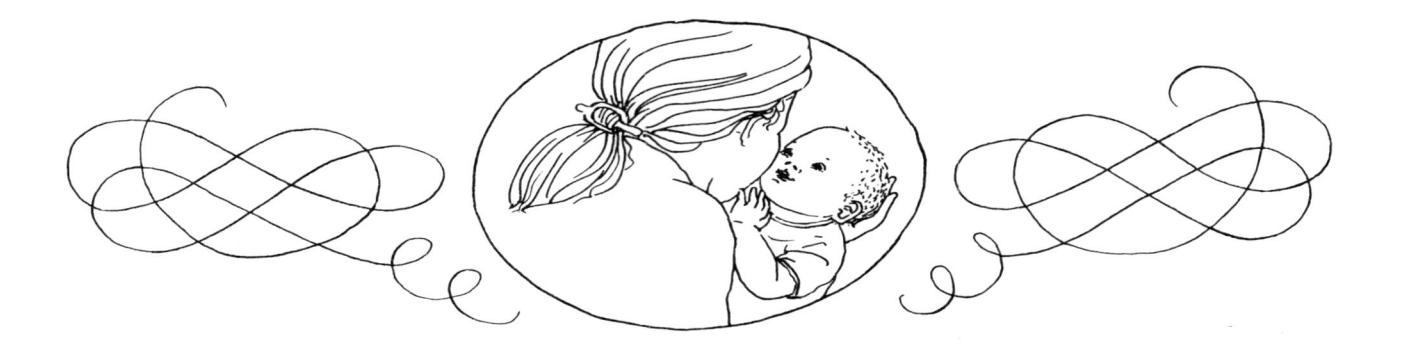

EDITOR'S NOTE The first few years of life are filled with precious moments that eventually blur into each other in our memories and do not even exist for the "grown-up" child. This record is intended for both parents. Perhaps it will help you to remember some special occasion that you will in turn be able to share with your child.

	Mother	Father
Were there any toys, books, records, places that you particularly enjoyed with your child? Any special games you played? Invented?	_____	_____
Did you have a "going to bed" ritual? Singing? Telling a story? Did you have a bathing ritual?	_____	_____
Record family reunions, special parties, family events (meeting theater or government personalities, or 25th or other wedding anniversaries)	_____	_____

RECORD 83 (CONTINUED)

Record here extraordinary events that your family survived—the Big Depression of 1932-1938, tornadoes, fires, wars, etc.

Record family achievements—books published, winning special prizes, building and selling a company you owned, etc.

How would you compare your own upbringing to that of your child's? Are you content with your efforts?

Did you bring up your child pretty much the same way you were brought up?

Other moments _____

Medical & Legal Records

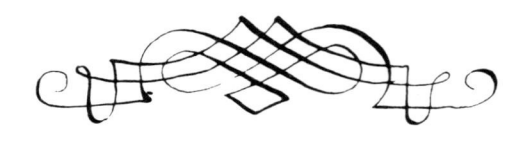

MEDICAL AND LEGAL RECORDS

Family Photo Tree and Family Medical Chart

EDITOR'S NOTE Who we are and where we came from are more than just names and dates. These data should also include a storehouse of information about the achievements and memories that make your family unique. Much information about individual members of the immediate family are included in previous pages devoted to mother, father, as well as your brothers and sisters. In the pages that follow, we make provision for a photo Family Tree and for recording father's and mother's ancestors as well as important medical information. Filling this out carefully can be a great asset to your offspring, especially when hereditary information is needed by your doctor to make an accurate diagnosis.

Instructions for Completing Family Photo Tree and Family Medical Chart

FAMILY PHOTO TREE

Insert photos in space provided on Record 84. Use a coin or stencil to cut photo and attach with spray adhesive or glue. Do not use rubber cement; with time, it discolors photo. Include full name of relative.

FAMILY MEDICAL CHART

Write in space provided on Record 85 the full name of each relative and in brackets the numbers that indicate relative's hereditary and medical history (see listing on this page).

    Example: <u>Marie Wilson, (3, 13, 22)</u>
                    aunt

On the next line, indicate the birthdate and, if appropriate, date of death. For aunts and uncles, list the full name of spouse on the first line.

Diseases

1. Allergies
2. Anemia
3. Arthritis
4. Baldness
5. Cancer (specify type)
6. Cerebral Palsy
7. Chromosomal Abnormalities (Down's Syndrome)
8. Cleft Lip or Palate
9. Club Foot
10. Congenital Heart Defect
11. Cystic Fibrosis
12. Diabetes
13. Epilepsy
14. Glaucoma
15. Hearing Loss
16. Hemophilia
17. Hernia
18. Hydrocephalus
19. Mental Illness (depression)
20. Mental Retardation
21. Metabolic Disorders
22. Migraine Headaches
23. Minimal Brain Dysfunction
24. Muscular Dystrophy
25. Obesity
26. PKU (Phenylketonuria)
27. Pyloric Stenosis
28. Prostate
29. Rh Disease
30. Rubella (German Measles)
31. Short Stature
32. Sickle-cell Anemia
33. Speech
34. Tumors
35. Varicose Veins
36. Visual Defects
37. Sterility
38. _____
39. _____
40. _____

Family Photo Tree

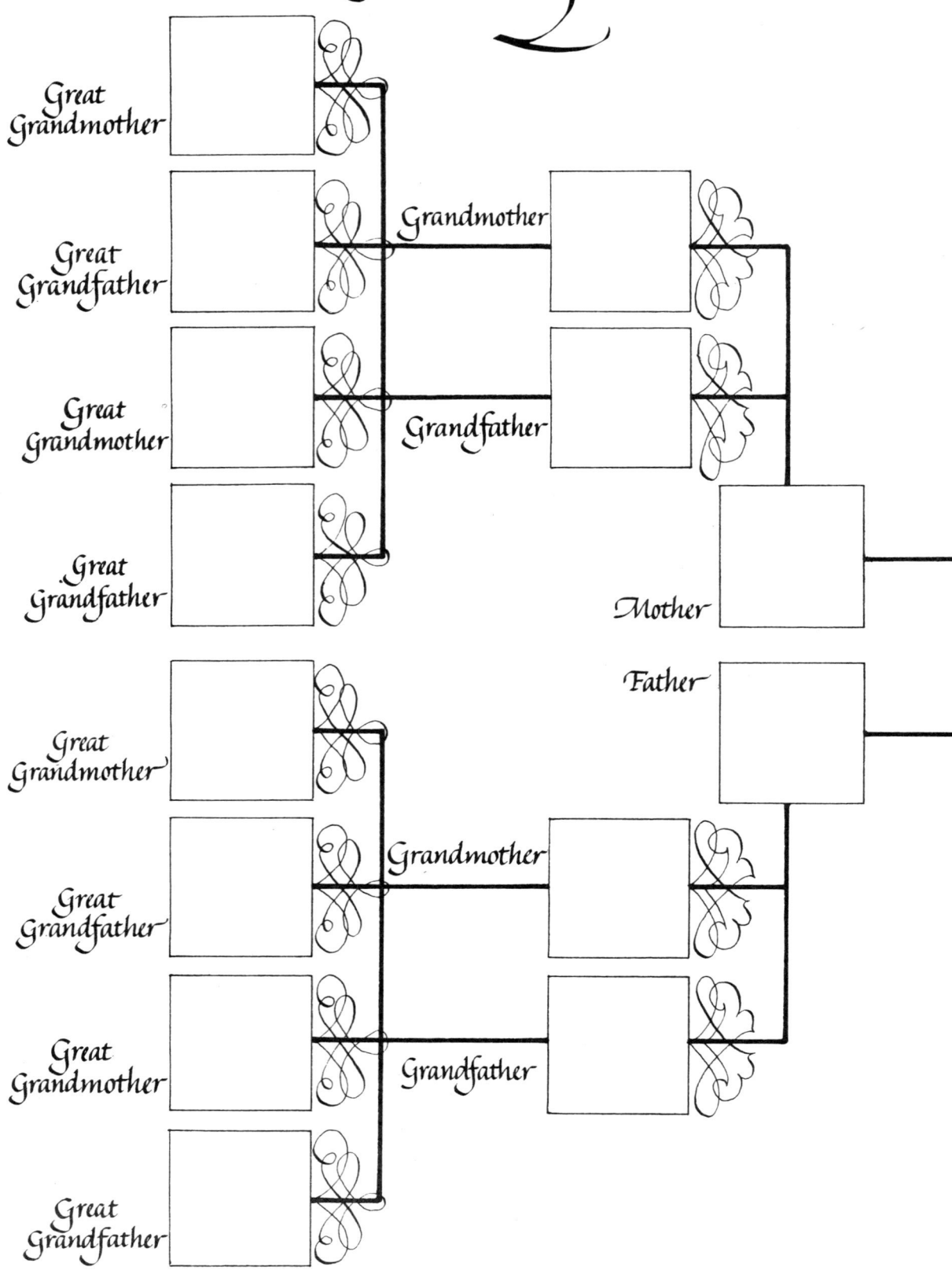

Great Grandmother

Great Grandfather

Grandmother

Great Grandmother

Great Grandfather

Mother

Father

Great Grandmother

Great Grandfather

Grandmother

Great Grandmother

Great Grandfather

Grandfather

Grandfather

		Cousins
Aunt		

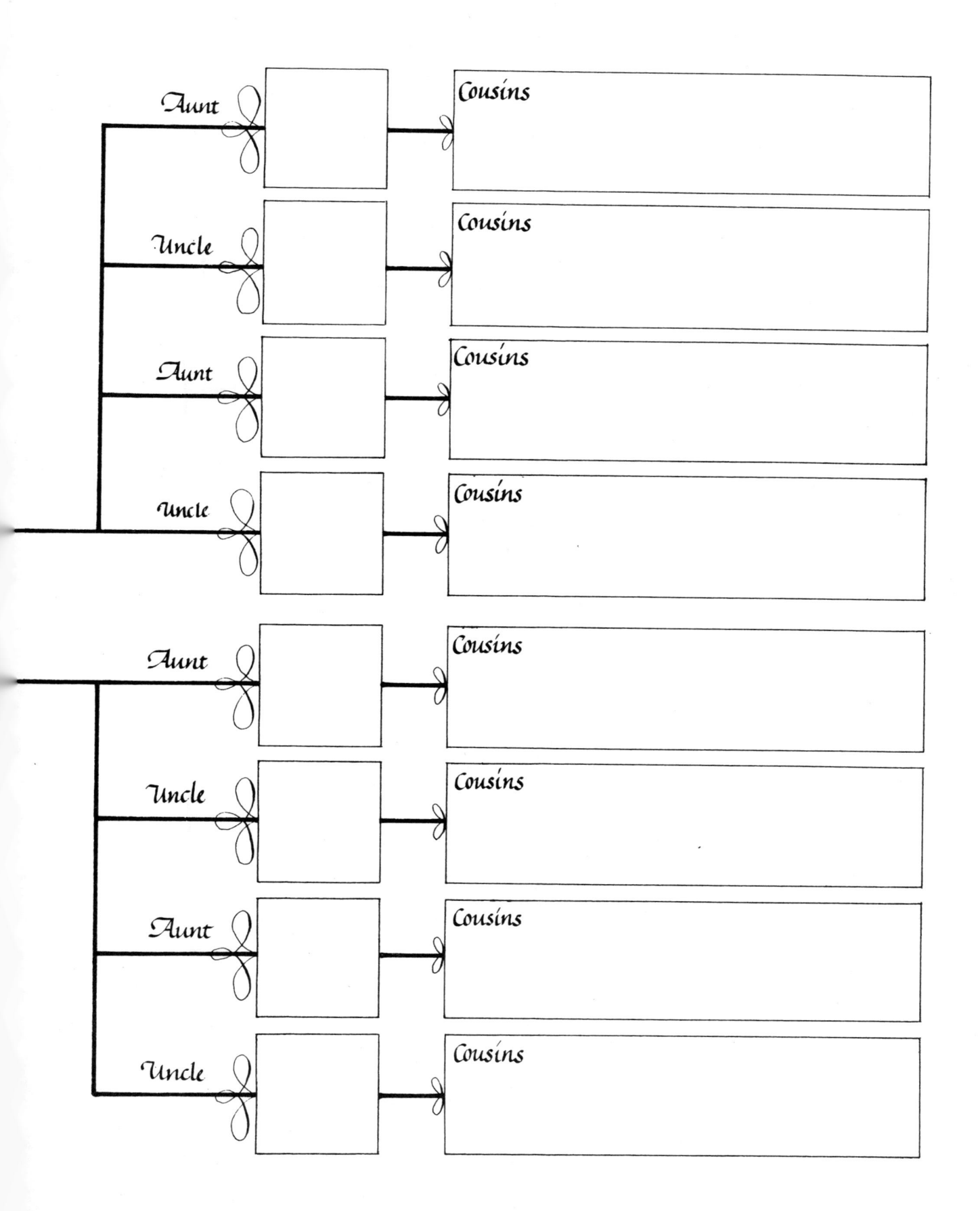

		Cousins
Uncle		

		Cousins
Aunt		

		Cousins
Uncle		

		Cousins
Aunt		

		Cousins
Uncle		

		Cousins
Aunt		

		Cousins
Uncle		

Family Medical Chart

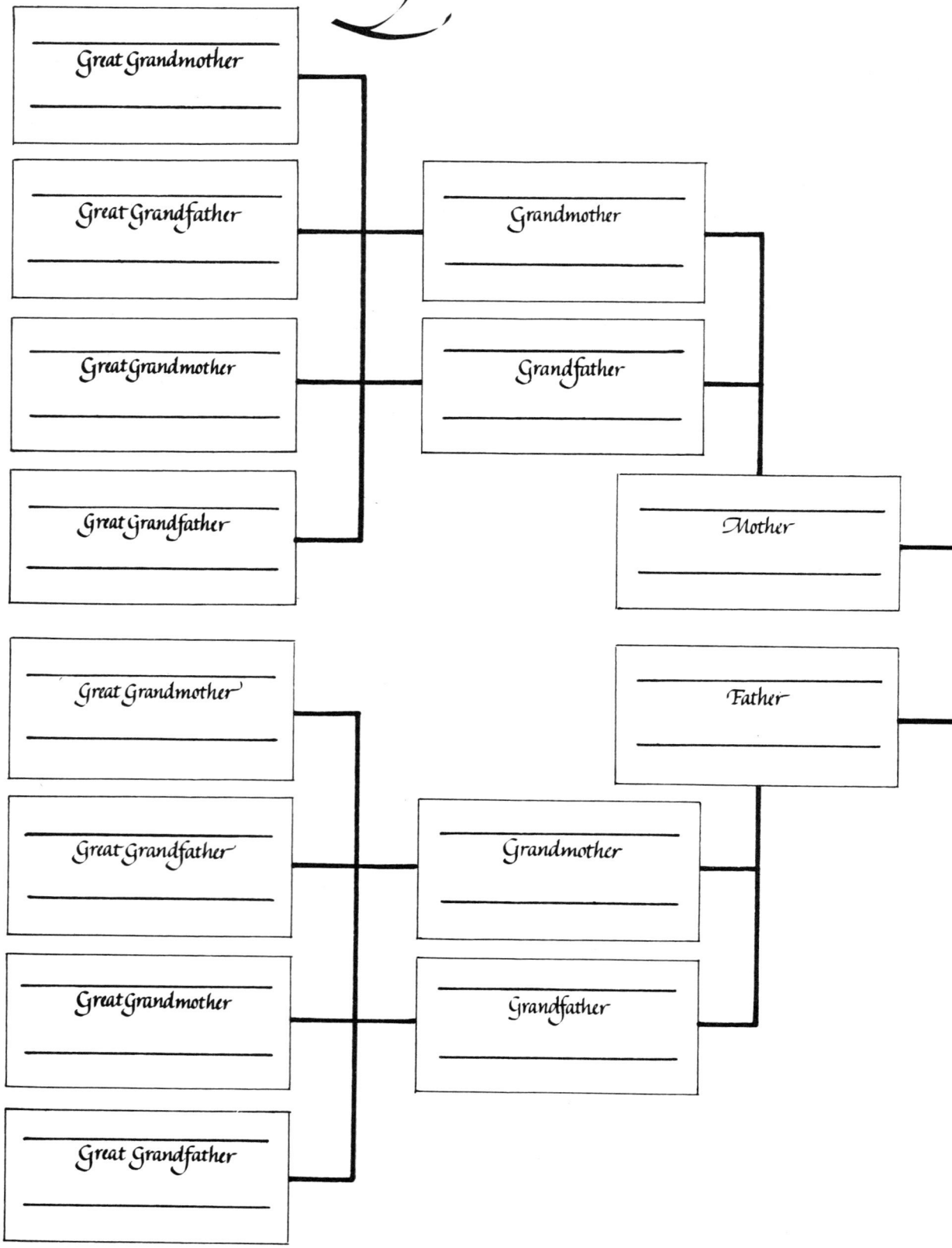

- Great Grandmother
- Great Grandfather
- Great Grandmother
- Great Grandfather
- Grandmother
- Grandfather
- Mother
- Great Grandmother
- Great Grandfather
- Great Grandmother
- Great Grandfather
- Grandmother
- Grandfather
- Father

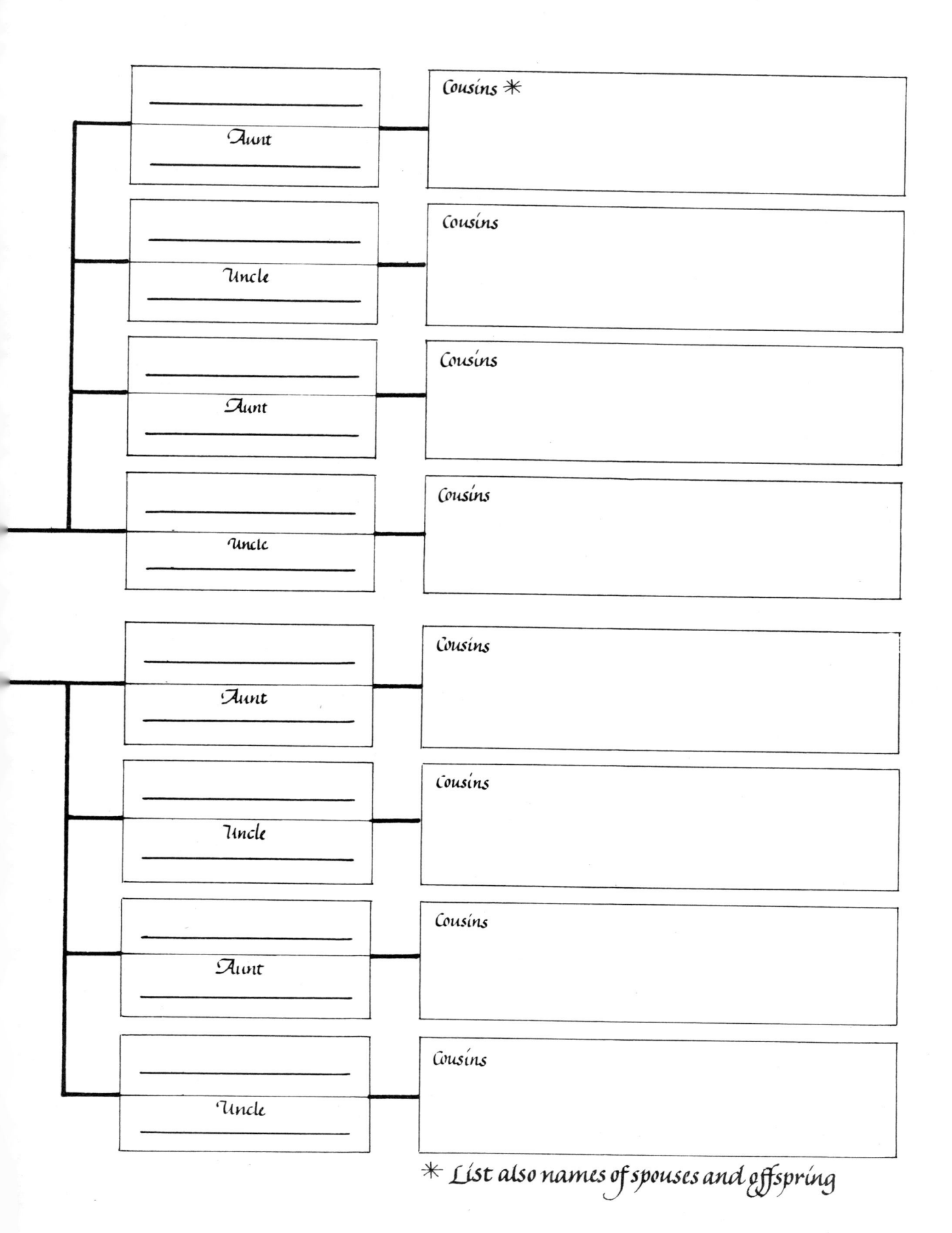

Aunt	Cousins *
Uncle	Cousins
Aunt	Cousins
Uncle	Cousins
Aunt	Cousins
Uncle	Cousins
Aunt	Cousins
Uncle	Cousins

✲ *List also names of spouses and offspring*

RECORD 86   Recorder _____

Allergy History

EDITOR'S NOTE Allergy is a symptomatic response to some aspect of the environment. Common allergic conditions are: hay fever, eczema, hives, persistent cough, runny, stuffy nose, asthma, wheezing. Causes of allergy usually are: something you eat, something you breathe, weather change, something you touch, infection, emotional factors.

First Symptoms	Onset Date	Suspected and Verified Causes	Treatment Used	Treatment Dates

Illnesses and X-rays

EDITOR'S NOTE This record will provide a complete medical history of your growing child. It will also give a physician access to X-rays already taken. This will save you money and, more importantly, avoid the harmful effects of repeating unnecessary X-rays.

RECORD OF ILLNESSES

Illness	Date	Severity/Complications/Treatment	Attending Doctor

RECORD 87 (CONTINUED)

RECORD OF X-RAYS AND TREATMENTS

Organ or Structure	Date	Taken at	Where	Diagnosis and Treatment by Doctor

Hospital Admissions

EDITOR'S NOTE Sometimes it is necessary to go to the hospital for exams and tests that cannot be made in doctors' offices. Keeping a record of your child's hospital admissions would be most useful if illness were to strike again. Keep a record of each admission and other information you think will be useful and important. Your doctor will then be able to locate your records without delay.

Date	Hospital	Address	City	Zip

Reason: _____
_____

Date	Hospital	Address	City	Zip

Reason: _____
_____

Date	Hospital	Address	City	Zip

Reason: _____
_____

Date	Hospital	Address	City	Zip

Reason: _____
_____

Date	Hospital	Address	City	Zip

Reason: _____
_____

Date	Hospital	Address	City	Zip

Reason: _____
_____

Date	Hospital	Address	City	Zip

Reason: _____
_____

Child's Accidents and Surgery

NON-OPERATIVE (Accidents/Injuries/Corrections)

Type	Date	Cause	Stay in Hospital	Child's Reaction	Behavioral Change (if any)	Doctor

RECORD OF SURGERY

Date	Surgery	Time Under Anesthesia	Surgeon	Results	Recuperative Period

RECORD 90   Recorder _____   239

Accidents, Negligence, Court Claims

EDITOR'S NOTE In our highly technical society in which sixteen-year-olds drive cars and other motorized vehicles, brakes do not always hold, and motorbikes are not licensed, a child and the parents are likely to have had at least one scuffle with the law. If any injuries are sustained, lawyers and doctors are involved and both parents need legal aid. Even after settlements are made, old injuries and side effects can reappear in later life and result in further litigation. Information about old injuries can become very important to your child. (Make one or two copies for your own records.)

Accidents in Your Child's Life:

Accident (describe) _____

_____

_____

_____

Who was responsible? _____

Property Damaged (yours and claimant's) _____

_____

Other Party _____
              Name

_____
            Address

Out-of-court Financial Settlement _____

Lawyer Consulted _____
            Name   Address   City   State   Zip

Medical Treatment:

Injuries Sustained (describe) _____

_____

Permanent Injuries (if any) _____

_____

_____

_____

_____

RECORD 90 (CONTINUED)

Medical Costs:

Hospital Costs _____

Hospital _____
        Name   Address   City   State   Zip

Surgical Costs _____

Surgeon _____
        Name   Address   City   State   Zip

Outpatient Costs or Treatment _____

Family Doctor _____
        Name   Address   City   State   Zip

X-rays Taken _____

_____

Location of These X-rays _____

Legal and Insurance Actions:

Lawyer Consulted _____
        Name   Address   City   State   Zip

Was child or parent or both sued for negligence?_____

_____

Legal Actions Commenced _____

In what court? _____

Did child testify as a witness? _____

Out-of-court or In-court Settlement, if any (describe) _____

_____

Insurance Paid _____

Insurance Company _____
        Name   Address   City   State   Zip

Insurance Company Agent _____
        Name   Address   City   State   Zip

RECORD 91   Recorder _____   241

Citizenship Record

EDITOR'S NOTE At some time in your child's life, she will be seeking a job, applying for admission to the bar, serving military duty, applying for a passport, or providing naturalization papers for citizenship or voting. She will need information that will require the parents' help to recall events in early as well as later years. Here is important personal data that most parents need to record.

CITIZENSHIP

All persons born or naturalized in the United States and subject to the jurisdiction thereof are citizens. Your child can acquire citizenship by virtue of *birth* in the United States or its possessions, or by going through a legal process (taking three to five years) called *naturalization*. Citizenship in the United States is a precious right to parent and child alike and must be carefully guarded from revocation.

Having and updating records of citizenship is a must!

Make a copy of your citizenship papers and include them in a Manila envelope with other important documents.

Citizenship by Virtue of Birth (check)

_____ Birth in U.S.A.

  Name of hospital or home address _____

  City _____ State _____

_____ Born on an American ship (flying the U.S. flag)

  Name of vessel _____ Date of travel _____

_____ Born in outlying U.S. possession with one parent a citizen

  Name of parent who was a citizen _____

RECORD 91 (CONTINUED)

_____ *Citizenship Attained by Naturalization*

Citizenship attained by parent (full name) _____

How long prior to child's birth did parent reside in U.S.A. or U.S. possession?

_____

_____ Born outside the U.S.A. or in a possession, with one parent a resident of U.S.A. for periods totaling ten years

Where? _____

How long did parent live in U.S.A.? _____

_____ *Citizenship via Naturalization of Parents*

Derivative citizenship from two naturalized parents

Name and address of court _____

Name of father; date and number of naturalization certificate:

_____

Name of mother; date and number of naturalization certificate:

_____

Does child hold dual nationality (citizenship in two countries)?

List country other than U.S.A. _____

Court in which child's derivative citizenship certificate was issued:

_____

Number and date of child's derivative citizenship certificate:

_____

Photo

Wills, Inheritances, and Legal Guardianship

EDITOR'S NOTE Death in a family always brings on crises, some of which may be mitigated to some extent by preplanning. Apart from emotional shock when one parent (or both) dies suddenly, there are problems in carrying out the deceased's wishes, closing a thriving business, locating wills and bank accounts, administering an estate, selecting legal guardians, protecting children from third parties who might try to profit from or distort the wishes of the deceased. Discriminating disposition of a lifetime collection of art, antiques, fine books, etc. requires careful screening and handling by specialists and cannot be delegated to children. Most parents do not like to talk to their children about wills, trust accounts, business assets, insurance, and personal and family property. To prepare for an orderly transfer to children, your answers to the questions below are one way of communicating your desires for the future of your children.

Wills:

Does a will exist? _____ Who has a copy of it? _____
                                                         Name
Address _____

Is there a copy in the house? _____ Where is it located? _____
Who drafted the will? _____
Do you have a lawyer whom both father and mother trust? _____

Name	Address	City	State	Zip

Name and address of person (executor of the will) you designate to manage the estate of husband or wife _____

Guardianship of your child _____
_____

Are both previous designations clearly specified in the will? _____

RECORD 92 (CONTINUED)

If either or both parents die or if accidental death befalls your child or children, who will the ultimate contingent beneficiary be? _____

Assets:

Banks (list banks and account numbers)
_____
_____
_____
_____
_____
_____

Loans unpaid _____
_____
_____
_____

Royalties due either parent from writing, design, or invention patents _____
_____
_____

Trust accounts or property that father or mother inherited from their parents (your grandparents). Describe fully, including location of grandparents' wills, etc. _____
_____
_____
_____

Personal property owned jointly or individually by either parent (list houses, land, etc.)
_____
_____
_____
_____
_____
_____
_____
_____

RECORD 92 (CONTINUED)

What life insurance do the parents own?

Mother _____

_____

_____

_____

_____

Father _____

_____

_____

_____

_____

Which charitable or educational organizations that have received your support do you wish your children to continue supporting if extra funds are available? _____

_____

_____

_____

Describe the use you wish your children and their children to make of their inheritance from you.

Appendix

Parents have a concerned interest in recording and measuring the early sensory achievements and physical movements of their newborn infant. They want to know if the behaviors are normal, whether their baby is average, ahead of his age level, etc. Whereas measurements in the area of language (after three years) may indicate IQ ability, they are not reliable in assessing nonverbal children, and they certainly do not measure creativity, drive, social competence, and self-image, all of which may be of even greater importance in later life.

However, infant-behavior researchers, psychologists, and educators are beginning to gather data that indicate a response pattern that could predict the type of adult he could become. Researchers with sophisticated electronic monitors and computers are studying patterns of "attending" (the manner in which infants respond to varying stimuli). Dr. Lewis Lipsitt of Brown University is researching the newborn's response to sensory stimuli (smell, taste, sight, and sound), which is especially important to the detection of possible nervous system malfunctions. This type of research is also helping to determine what kind of home or laboratory stimulation is necessary to bring forth an "intellectually alive" child, one who will be able to cope with the complexities of reading, mathematics, etc.

Tests for infants and preschoolers are usually administered by psychologists and educators. Test publishers have recently begun to explore parent-administered tests. Most of these tests are quite lengthy (eight- to sixteen-page pamphlets), with intricate instructions and complicated scoring systems that only a professional can understand. Because of space limitations, we have summarized these tests in a few pages and deliberately left out the scoring procedures. Filling out each digested version is intended only to alert parents to their existence, and to enable them to add the results to their child's data bank. We hope the tests will serve as a "behavior inventory" and learning device for interested parents.

We have also included tests that only professionals can administer. These should be Xeroxed and left with each particular professional to fill out. When filled out, return them to this book by stapling each record onto the page from which it was taken. Some of these tests will convey to your adolescent child a picture of positive and negative childhood behaviors and family circumstances. All of the information will be useful.

Your diligence in filling out the questionnaires will give your adult offspring a better understanding of himself and the values of life he learned from both parents.

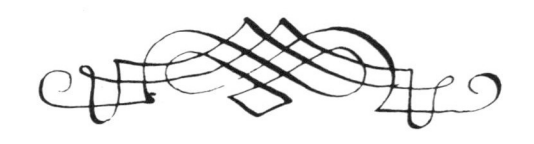

APPENDIX

Denver Developmental Screening Test
(A Professional Record)

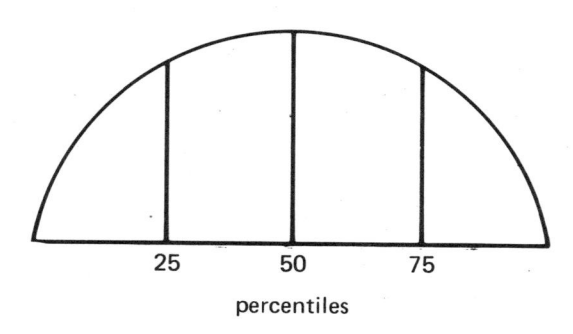

25 50 75
percentiles

EVALUATION OF GROWTH AND DEVELOPMENT*

Each baby is a unique individual. Her growth and development should not be compared with her brother's and sister's, nor the neighbor's children. Illustrated here is a diagram of the normal distribution curve along which growth and development take place.

The 25th percentile for weight, for example, means that 75 percent of the children of the same age will weigh more than she does and 25 percent will weigh less. The 75th percentile for weight means that 25 percent of the children of the same age will weigh more than she does and 75 percent will weigh less. The presence of your baby in the 10th percentile or 90th percentile does not indicate that anything is wrong. If a baby's growth and development fall at either end of this distribution curve, they are not average *but still within normal limits.*

The percentile into which your baby falls at birth will probably remain constant in spite of growth and development. This is frequently charted, and if a marked change occurs, diagnostic studies may be indicated. One of the most important reasons for monthly well-baby visits is to allow your physician to evaluate your baby's growth and development. This is best done on a continuing basis, and the evaluation must take into consideration *all* her abilities. For example, a two-and-one-half-year-old who does not walk and talk may be perfectly normal. The average age at which to look for specific development is given below. If parents have doubts they should consult their doctor.

The American Academy of Pediatrics has recommended to physicians the Denver Developmental Screening Test, which is intended to detect developmental delays. It is administered to the so-called normal child at one year of age as a screening procedure. *It is not an intelligence test.* The test helps detect hearing loss, minor brain damage, and other conditions that are not obvious to either the doctor or parent. This type of record keeping helps parents to see the "ages and stages" of normal development and to dispell any fears they may have about any "peculiar" behaviors of their child.

*This record was prepared by the Denver Medical School and is usually filled out by doctors. However, only parents have the time or interest to follow their child's development from month to month. Parts of this inventory are included in other records.

RECORD 93 (CONTINUED)

The Newborn.
The baby sucks, swallows, and roots at birth. (Rooting means that when the infant smells milk, he turns his head to find the source, and that when the cheek is touched by a smooth object, his mouth turns toward the object and his lips open as if to grasp a nipple.) Purposeless movements are characteristic of this age. A sneezing reflex is present. A newborn baby can immediately tell light from dark, but he cannot focus clearly enough to recognize people. He distinguishes people by the way they handle him and talk to him.

First Month.
In general, an infant's motor development takes place from head to toe.
1. She can raise her head from the surface while in a prone position, as well as regard your face while you are in her direct line of vision.
2. She responds to loud noises.
3. She will flinch at a bright light.
4. She learns to recognize familiar voices.
5. She can taste and smell.
6. She begins to make small throaty sounds.
7. The tonic neck reflex is present. It is characterized by three components:
    (a) the head is turned far to the side
    (b) one arm is extended on the same side
    (c) the other arm is bent close to the shoulder.
8. Her hands will clench a rattle on contact, but she immediately drops it.
9. Placed in a supported sitting position, her head sags forward; the back is evenly rounded.
10. When pulled to the sitting position there is marked lagging of the head.
11. She can move around a little bit, enough to squirm to the corner of the crib.

Second Month.
1. He will look at objects.
2. He follows a moving person.
3. He may smile.
4. He makes cooing sounds.
5. He makes single vowel sounds, such as "ah," "eh," "uh."
6. He may be able to grasp a rattle for a short period of time.
7. When held, he will have control of his neck; it will jerk and bob, but no longer sag forward.

Third Month.
1. Head control is markedly improved.
2. She will focus on brightly colored objects and follow their movements from side to side.
3. Salivation becomes active. This is confused with teething by many parents.
4. She will definitely respond to you. When you smile, she will probably coo and smile back.
5. She will raise her chest by pushing up on her arms.
6. In sitting, however, her back is still rounded.
7. Thrashing movements of the arms and legs are common.
8. She may choose a favorite position for sleeping.

Fourth Month.

The baby's personality now becomes apparent.
 1. He will turn his head toward voices.
 2. He becomes skilled at focusing his eyes on brightly colored objects.
 3. A laugh has developed.
 4. There is the beginning of co-ordination between his eyes and body movements.
 5. He looks down at the tabletop and at his hands.
 6. The fingers touch and play with each other.
 7. He may discover he can use fingers separately.
 8. He regards a rattle in his hand.
 9. His hands engage in front of him.
 10. There is exploration of his surroundings.
 11. When held upright, he will extend his legs and support some weight.
 12. He will sit propped up for 10 to 15 minutes. This will not hurt his back. This fear probably originated when rickets was common.
 13. He anticipates feeding on sight of food.
 14. He is on the verge of rolling over.

Fifth Month.

She discovers new things about her environment and her own body.
 1. Everything automatically goes into the mouth.
 2. There is much drooling.
 3. She talks to herself when alone.
 4. She drops a toy and will follow it with her eyes.
 5. She may try to catch moving objects between her hands.
 6. She pulls at her clothes.
 7. She can sit erect with support. Her back is now straighter.
 8. She will roll over for the first time. *Caution:* The baby will probably roll over for the first time when you least expect it. Never leave your baby unguarded on a bed or on any surface from which she can fall.
 9. She may appear afraid of strangers because she recognizes the difference between familiar and unfamiliar people.

Sixth Month.

 1. He will lift his chest up completely and support himself on his hands and knees.
 2. He will grasp objects and possibly transfer an object from one hand to the other.
 3. He will possibly pick up objects from the crib.
 4. He will move toward objects.
 5. He may object when he loses a toy or is left alone. This represents an increased interest in the world around him.
 6. He is more sociable; he will look up from what he is doing when people enter the room.

RECORD 93 (CONTINUED)

Sixth to Ninth Months.
1. She lifts her head while lying on her back.
2. She puts her toes into her mouth.
3. She will say certain words, such as "Ma-ma" and "Da-da."
4. She reaches with one hand.
5. She will transfer a ring from one hand to the other.
6. She will bang a bell.
7. She will pull herself up alone.
8. She will be able to sit alone.
9. She will be able to go from a sitting to a lying-down position.
10. The ability to creep usually develops after six months of age. The baby who creeps well may be a late walker if she is satisfied with her ability to move around. Some babies never creep, but only sit until they can stand, and then walk.
11. She will talk to her toys, chew toys, and will persistently reach for toys out of reach.
12. Placed before a mirror, she will smile and pat the glass.

Ninth to Twelfth Months.
1. He will stand with or without support.
2. He develops the ability to pick up things between the thumb and forefinger. This is called *prehensile ability.* It is the most useful way of using the hand.
3. He will probably start walking. (Some babies, however, will not walk until they are two or three years of age, and this is not necessarily abnormal.)
4. He will show more independence.
5. He may insist upon holding his spoon at meals.
6. He will drink from a cup.
7. He may be reluctant to go to sleep because he does not want to be separated from his parents.
8. He will begin to learn the meaning of the word "No" and to understand simple commands.
9. He imitates sounds—e.g., coughing.
10. He responds to his name.
11. He will roll or throw a ball.
12. He will offer a ball to you, but not release it.
13. He will grasp a bell by its handle.
14. He will pull on a string.
15. He will relinquish a toy on request.
16. He will attempt to build a tower with blocks without success.
17. He will co-operate in dressing.
18. He will play "pat-a-cake" and "bye-bye."
19. He will place two cubes together.
20. He will place a cube in a cup.
21. He will try to insert a pellet in a bottle, with success.

Twelfth to Eighteenth Months.
1. She will use a spoon well.
2. She will use groups of words with gestures.
3. She will sit in a small chair without assistance.

RECORD 93 (CONTINUED)

  4. She seldom falls when walking.
  5. She will climb stairs.
  6. She will run.
  7. She hurls a ball.
  8. She will turn pages of a book.
  9. She will put blocks in a hole.
10. She will imitate strokes with a crayon.
11. She identifies one picture.
12. She builds a tower of three blocks.
13. She pulls a toy.
14. On command she will put a toy on a chair.
15. She plays with and carries about a stuffed animal.
16. She hands the empty dish to her mother.

Two Years.
  1. He points to his eyes, nose, and mouth.
  2. He imitates circular strokes.
  3. He kicks a ball.
  4. He turns pages singly.
  5. He identifies three to five pictures.
  6. He feeds his stuffed animal.
  7. He builds a tower of seven blocks.
  8. He aligns cubes.
  9. He uses three- to four-word sentences.
10. He asks for food and drink.
11. He asks to go to the toilet.
12. He verbalizes his immediate experience, referring to himself by name.
13. He carries out simple commands on request.
14. He often squats to play on the floor.

Three Years.
  1. She copies a circle.
  2. She matches three color forms.
  3. She builds a tower of ten blocks.
  4. She kicks a ball well.
  5. She jumps on both feet and can jump down from a height of five feet.
  6. She can walk on her tiptoes.
  7. She pulls on her shoe.
  8. She stands on one foot momentarily.
  9. She pedals a bicycle.
10. She unbuttons her clothing.
11. She pours liquid from a pitcher to a glass.
12. She feeds herself with little spilling.
13. Her vocabulary contains many words.
14. She gives her last name.

RECORD 94   Recorder _____   254

Breast-feeding Survey
(A Researcher's Record)

EDITOR'S NOTE *Breast-feeding was once the natural method of feeding babies and is being encouraged again today. The most current research indicates that breast-fed babies <u>and their mothers</u> are emotionally, physically, and nutritionally better off. This record is intended to follow the stages and details of breast-feeding and to indicate the interpersonal aspects associated with it.*

(Make additional copies for yourself to use with subsequent children, whether breast-fed or not. The comparison should be very revealing.)

Family Data

Mother's age at time of birth of baby _____ Number of prior children _____

Have you nursed other babies? _____ If so, for how long? _____

Why did you decide to breast-feed? reading _____ doctor _____

husband _____ friends _____ other _____

Did you consider it successful? for yourself _____ for baby _____

Why? _____
_____

For how many months did you totally breast-feed? _____

Phase One/The Process

Was the breast used for sucking as well as nutrition? _____

Did you use a pacifier? _____ If yes, when was it introduced? _____

How frequently? _____ When was it discontinued? _____

Did you use an occasional bottle? _____ If yes, when was it introduced? _____

How frequently? _____

Did you give your baby night breast-feedings? _____ If yes, for how long? _____

In what position did you nurse? _____ chair _____ lying down

Did you ever sleep with your baby? _____ If yes, explain the circumstances and frequency _____
_____

Were you working or studying outside the house at this time? _____

If yes, explain _____

Were you able to take the baby most places with you? _____

RECORD 94 (CONTINUED)

At what age did you first leave the baby at home? _____

For what reason? _____ For how long? _____

Did you nurse the baby on schedule? _____ By demand? _____

How frequently did you nurse? _____

Phase Two/Weaning

When did you first introduce the following: Solids _____ Which ones? _____

Water _____ Other liquids _____

At what age did you decide to wean the baby? _____ Did you hasten the process? _____

If yes, how? _____

Did you let the baby wean himself? _____

When did he show an interest in the cup? _____

Did frequency and nursing periods remain the same? _____ or decrease? _____

*Please make a copy of this record and send it to us at P.C.I., 306 Alexander St., Princeton, NJ 08540. We will forward it to researchers in this field.

RECORD 95   Recorder _____

Evaluation of Your Child's Learning and Development

FOR AGES THREE TO SIX YEARS
(A Professional Record)

EDITOR'S NOTE Records can indicate negative as well as positive behaviors. Not all children are "angels"; on occasion, some are "brats." Your child grown to adulthood might like to know the good, as well as the not-so-good, in her early life history. (You may want to have the teacher fill out a copy of this record.)

Name of child _____ Age of child _____

Speech: (circle number that best describes your child)
1 Makes no sounds.
2 Makes sounds but not understandable.
3 Speech very difficult to understand.
4 Speech somewhat difficult to understand.
5 Speech easily understood.

Vocabulary:
1 Is nearly nonverbal.
2 Asks for at least ten things by their appropriate names.
3 Uses names of familiar objects.
4 Names people or objects when describing pictures.
5 Talks about action when describing pictures.

Writing:
1 Cannot write or print any words.
2 Writes or prints own name.
3 Writes or prints ten words.
4 Writes or prints forty words.
5 Writes short notes and memos.
6 Writes sensible and understandable letters.

Dressing:
1 Does not co-operate in dressing by extending arms or legs.
2 Does not dress self but co-operates.
3 Partially dresses self, cannot zip or button.
4 Partially dresses self, can zip or button.
5 Completely dresses self, except tying shoes.
6 Completely dresses self.

RECORD 95 (CONTINUED)

Use of Table Utensils:
1. Must be fed.
2. Feeds self with fingers.
3. Feeds self with spoon—considerable spilling.
4. Feeds self with spoon—neatly.
5. Feeds self with spoon and fork—considerable spilling.
6. Feeds self with spoon and fork—neatly.
7. Uses table knife for cutting or spreading.
8. Uses knife and fork correctly and neatly.

Responsibility:
1. Not given responsibility; is unable to carry out responsibility at all.
2. Unreliable—makes little effort to carry out responsibility; one is uncertain that the assigned act will be performed.
3. Usually dependable—makes an effort to carry out responsibility—one can be reasonably certain that the assigned act will be performed.
4. Very conscientious and assumes much responsibility—makes a special effort, the assigned act will always be performed.

Initiative:
1. Does not engage in assigned activities—e.g., putting away toys, etc..
2. Will engage in activities only if assigned or directed.
3. Asks if there is something for him to do or explores surroundings—e.g., home, yard, etc..
4. Initiates most of his own activities—e.g., tasks, games, etc.

Maladaptive Behavior (1 = Never; 2 = Occasionally; 3 = Frequently)

_____ Threatens or does physical violence to others or to self.
_____ Damages own or other's property.
_____ Disrupts other's activities.
_____ Uses profane or hostile language.
_____ Is rebellious—e.g., ignores regulations, resists following instructions.
_____ Runs away or attempts to run away.
_____ Is untrustworthy—e.g., takes others' property, lies, cheats.
_____ Will not sit still for any length of time.
_____ Displays heterosexual and/or homosexual behavior that is socially unacceptable.

RECORD 96

Guide for Observing Motor Development

EDITOR'S NOTE *Back in the early 1930s, Myrtle B. McGraw, Ph.D. pioneered infant physical movement research, as did Dr. Arnold Gesell. We present here some of her early attempts to get parents to observe more carefully what is happening to an infant as he masters developmental motor sequences. The activities described are those of a normal baby. The specific age at which he acquires them is not important. However, the small changes from one level to another are, because they signal the development of the infant's brain and nervous system. Almost all the things he does during the first few weeks of life are reflexive and are controlled by the primitive part of the brain. After that, the human part of the brain takes over and starts to function with intentional behavior. This record will help you read your baby's signals.*

Response to Startle: The newborn lying quietly on her back in a relaxed manner has a startle reaction with all her muscles to the forceful blow of a stick or ruler on the side of the crib. As her brain develops, she learns to control such reactions. Below are the typical stages.

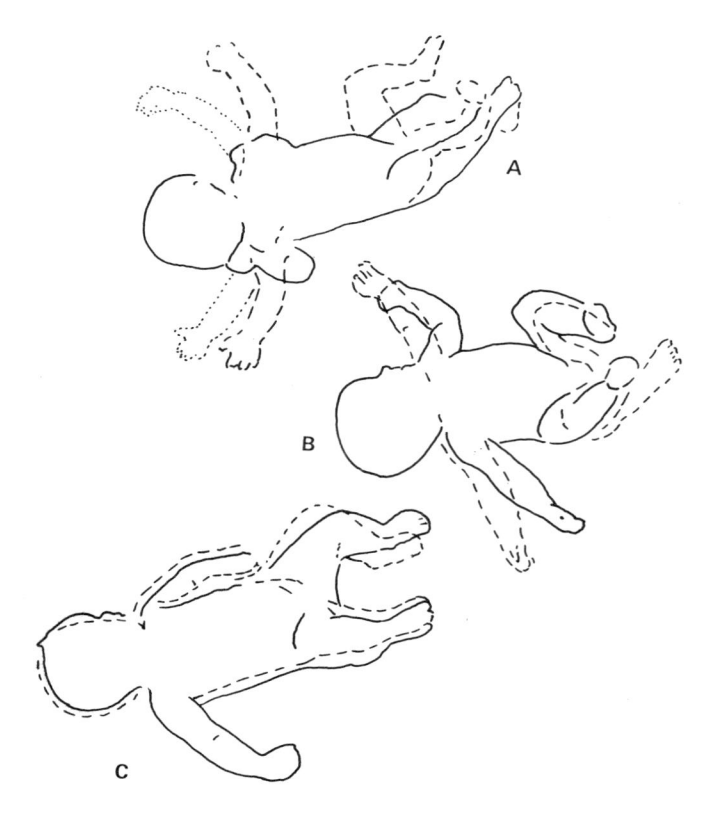

1. Note if both arms suddenly spring out from the shoulder and then form a bowing position over the chest. The legs flex and stiffen and straighten out. The baby may throw her head back and roll to one side (A).
   Date _____ Yes _____ No _____

2. The baby remains on her back, throws her arms out, but does not bring them together in bowing fashion (B).
   Date _____ Yes _____ No _____

3. The response becomes limited to a simple "body jerk" and "blinking" similar to an adult response and represents maturity of this activity (C).
   Date _____ Yes _____ No _____

RECORD 96 (CONTINUED)

Sitting: The ability to sit is a distinctly human trait (as against animals that squat on their haunches). In order to sit alone, the baby must be able to withstand the pull of gravity. To do this you take your baby's hands and pull her slowly into a sitting position. Pull her gently so she will exert her utmost muscular capacity. Watch the way she handles her head, trunk, and legs as she is being pulled upward. After she is in a sitting posture, place your hand on her back so you may feel the direction of the fall. In observing development of this activity, note the amount of effort your baby makes while being raised and her ability to prevent herself from falling after she has been placed in a sitting position.

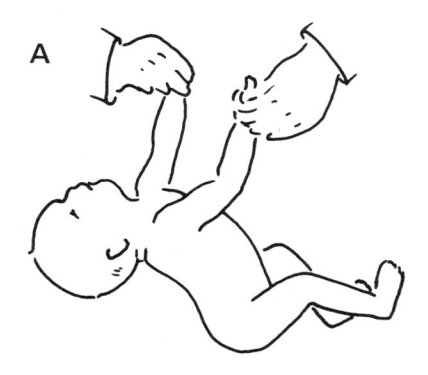

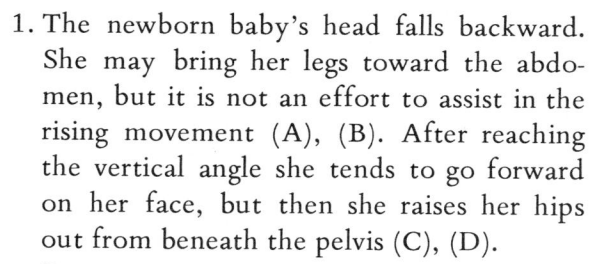

1. The newborn baby's head falls backward. She may bring her legs toward the abdomen, but it is not an effort to assist in the rising movement (A), (B). After reaching the vertical angle she tends to go forward on her face, but then she raises her hips out from beneath the pelvis (C), (D).
   Date_____Yes_____ No_____

2. During the rising movement, the baby holds her head in the same line as her trunk. If she is gently pushed forward she cannot free her legs and usually cries (B), (D).
   Date_____ Yes_____ No_____

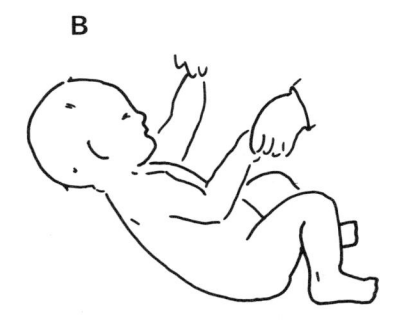

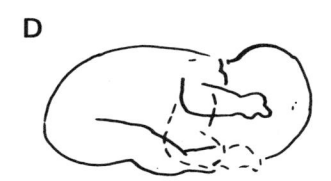

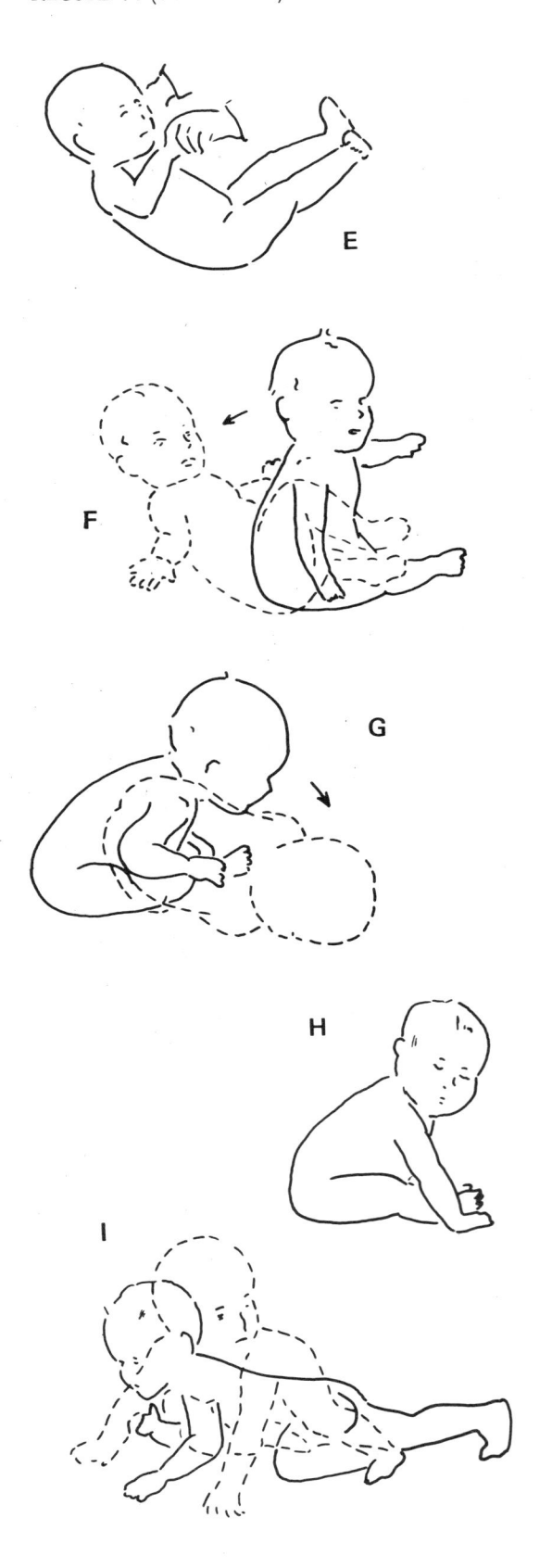

RECORD 96 (CONTINUED)

3. The baby exerts great effort in the rising movement. Give the minimum assistance in order to bring out the utmost effort (E).
Date _____ Yes _____ No _____

4. After being brought to the vertical angle, the baby tends to spring to the side or backwards (F, G). The baby sits for some moments, spine at an angle to the surface, supporting himself with arms and hands (H). The baby rolls over and then pushes into a sitting position (I).
Date _____ Yes _____ No _____

5. The baby can maintain his spine vertical to the surface and arms free for other activities (J). He has eliminated the roundabout way of rolling over preparatory to sitting. He turns slightly to one side and pushes up with his elbow (K). The baby is able to sit quite well on a flat surface, but he loses some control if brought to the edge of the table so that the lower legs are suspended over the edge.
Date _____ Yes _____ No _____

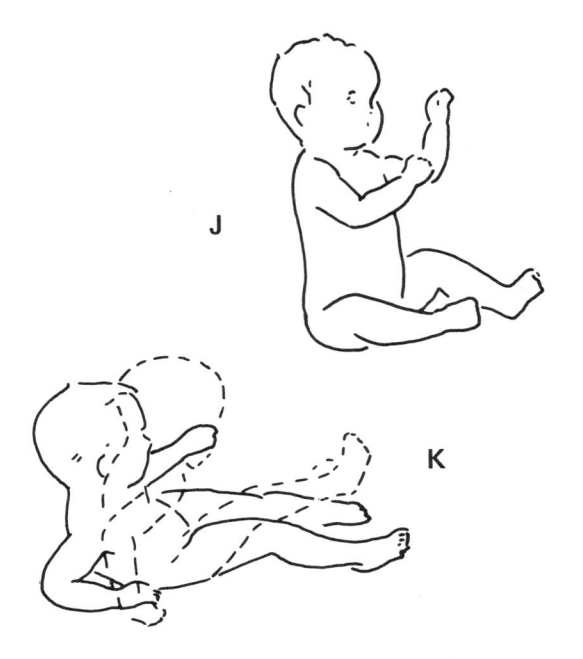

RECORD 96 (CONTINUED

Rolling Over: The ability to turn from the back on to the stomach is often misinterpreted by parents and less experienced observers. Parents sometimes report that the baby must have turned over at the age of two weeks because they found him on his stomach after having been placed on his back. This automatic "righting reflex" should not be confused with the ability to roll over that occurs later. Most babies are capable of righting themselves—i.e., turning from back to stomach soon after birth, but rolling over is a learned skill that comes in the fifth to ninth months.

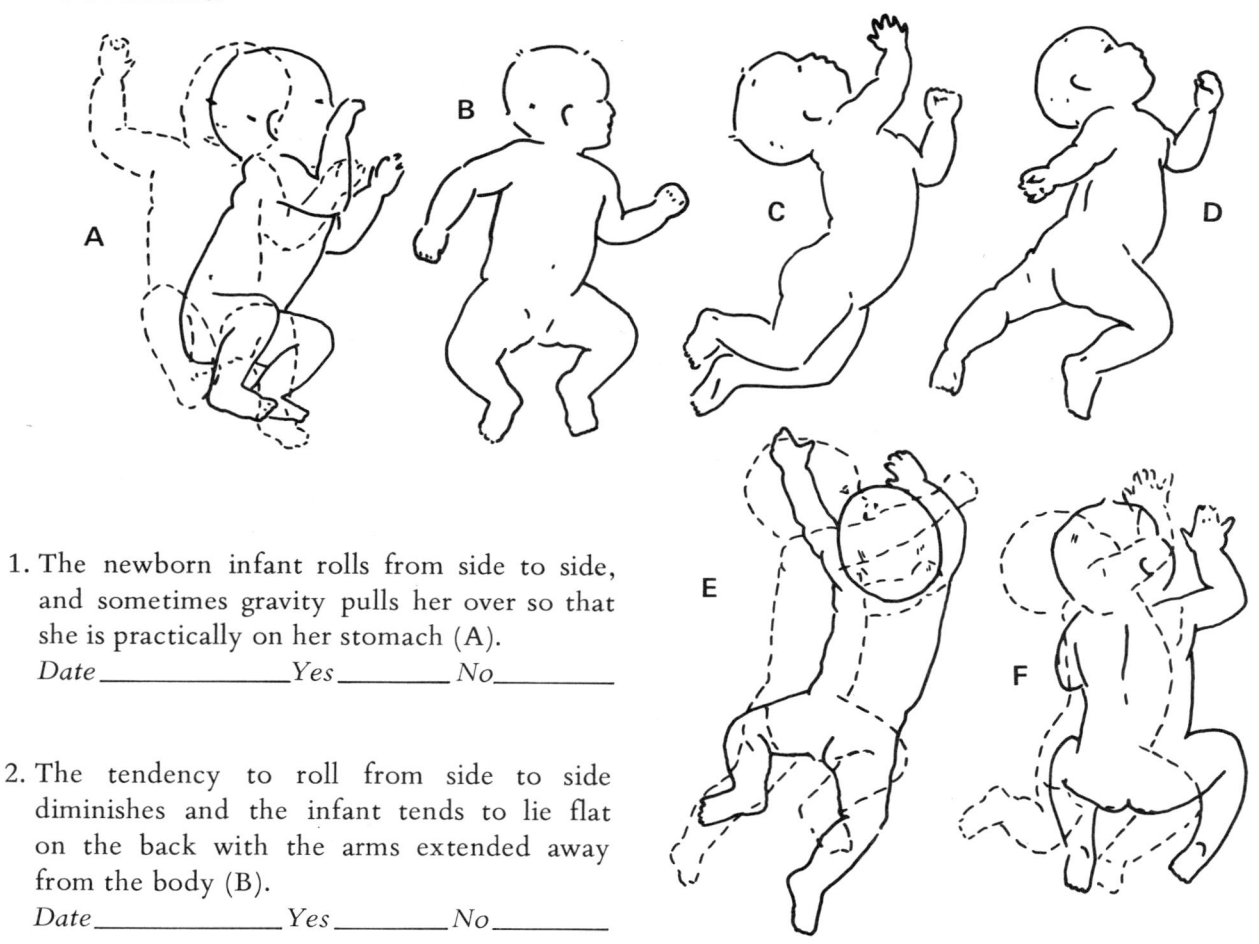

1. The newborn infant rolls from side to side, and sometimes gravity pulls her over so that she is practically on her stomach (A).
   Date_____ Yes_____ No_____

2. The tendency to roll from side to side diminishes and the infant tends to lie flat on the back with the arms extended away from the body (B).
   Date_____ Yes_____ No_____

3. The infant throws her head back, arches her spine, and attempts to roll over (C).
   Date_____ Yes_____ No_____

4. The baby starts the rolling movements by throwing the leg over and turning the hips, but is not able to complete the roll to a prone position (D).
   Date_____ Yes_____ No_____

5. The infant successfully turns from back to stomach and can free the arms beneath the chest (E).
   Date_____ Yes_____ No_____

6. The infant easily and smoothly rolls from back to stomach and then pushes up on hands and knees. The development of this activity is preparatory to the emergence of creeping, or getting into a sitting position (F).
   Date_____ Yes_____ No_____

Observing Eye-hand Co-ordination
(AS DEVELOPED BY DR. MYRTLE B. McGRAW)

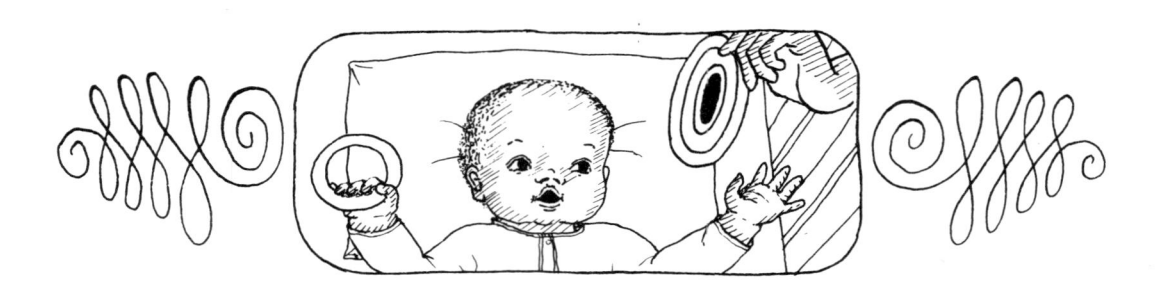

EDITOR'S NOTE A great step forward in the evolution of human beings occurred when our forelimbs were no longer a necessary tool for progression. Our hands became freed for other activities. In the human infant, development of the ability to reach for and handle objects is dependent upon eye and hand relations. Experts are not in total agreement about the status of infant vision. Certainly the wide-eyed, steady gaze can give parents the feeling that the baby is "taking it all in." You know that if you put something in the palm of his hand, he will clamp down on it tightly. Grasping and vision appear to be independent in the early weeks of life. In this section you will find some suggestions for observing the interaction of these two functions and the developmental changes.

1. When you move an object about the size of a stopwatch within the baby's visual range, his eyes may track the movement of the object, but he makes no attempt to bring his arms toward the object. At times the tracking of the object may lag behind the moving object. You can also test for accommodation to distance. Move the object slowly up and down above his face and note if his eyes turn toward his nose when the object is near.
   Date _____ Yes _____ No _____

2. The baby begins to spread her fingers somewhat and move both arms toward the object as soon as it is brought within her visual range.
   Date _____ Yes _____ No _____

3. The infant spreads his fingers and moves both arms to grasp the object. This is a fairly automatic or compulsive type of reaching pattern. Any object tends to bring forth this response.
   Date _____ Yes _____ No _____

4. The baby not only takes the object, but as she looks at it she turns it around, inspecting it or manipulating it in some way.
   Date _____ Yes _____ No _____

RECORD 97 (CONTINUED)

From now on, watch for gradual improvement in your infant's efficiency at reaching. He will still tend to keep his eyes fixed on the object, but will delay spreading arms and fingers until the hand is closer to the object. The baby will begin to be able to judge better just how much he needs to open the fingers in order to grasp different objects. (Note the difference between the way an adult picks up various objects and the way an infant does.)

5. The baby begins to pick up small objects between his thumb and index finger without trying to wrap all his fingers around them.
    Date _____ Yes _____ No _____

6. The baby can take one glance at an object, then continue moving her hand to pick it up even when her glance is directed elsewhere. In other words, the eyes and the hand are not glued to each other in order for the baby to carry out the act of picking up an object.
    Date _____ Yes _____ No _____

7. Let the baby see you place an object on the table. Then immediately cover it with a cloth. The baby makes no effort to retrieve it—"out of sight, out of mind."
    Date _____ Yes _____ No _____

8. When the baby sees the cover placed over the object, he immediately and directly pulls the cloth aside and picks up the object.
    Date _____ Yes _____ No _____

RECORD 98

Observation Guide on Standing

EDITOR'S NOTE *To become mobile, the infant needs to acquire not only the ability to walk on two feet, but must first be able to get up from a reclining position unaided. Normally one waits until the baby spontaneously pulls herself up by the side of the crib. However, if while your baby is lying on her back, you take her hands and gently pull upward, you will from the start be able to train yourself to give the minimum assistance in order to have your child exert the utmost effort.*

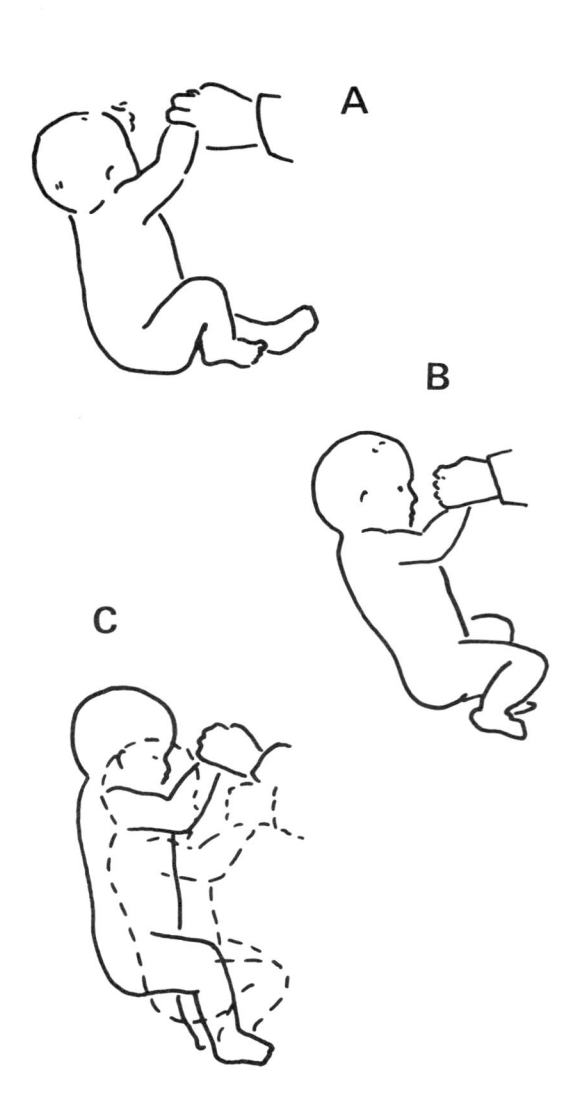

1. After the baby has been pulled to a sitting angle give an additional little pull upward. She makes no effort to place her feet on the bed to push up (A).
   Date _____ Yes _____ No _____

2. After being pulled up toward the sitting position, the baby puts his feet on the surface of the bed, raises his buttocks a little, but does not straighten his legs (B).
   Date _____ Yes _____ No _____

3. As you pull the infant gently you can feel her push against the surface and spring to a standing position, not completely erect (C).
   Date _____ Yes _____ No _____

4. After the baby has pushed up to a standing position (i.e., the leaning-backward position), he steps back with one foot in order to bring his shoulders above the hips (D).
   Date _____ Yes _____ No _____

*Developed by Dr. Myrtle B. McGraw.

RECORD 98 (CONTINUED)

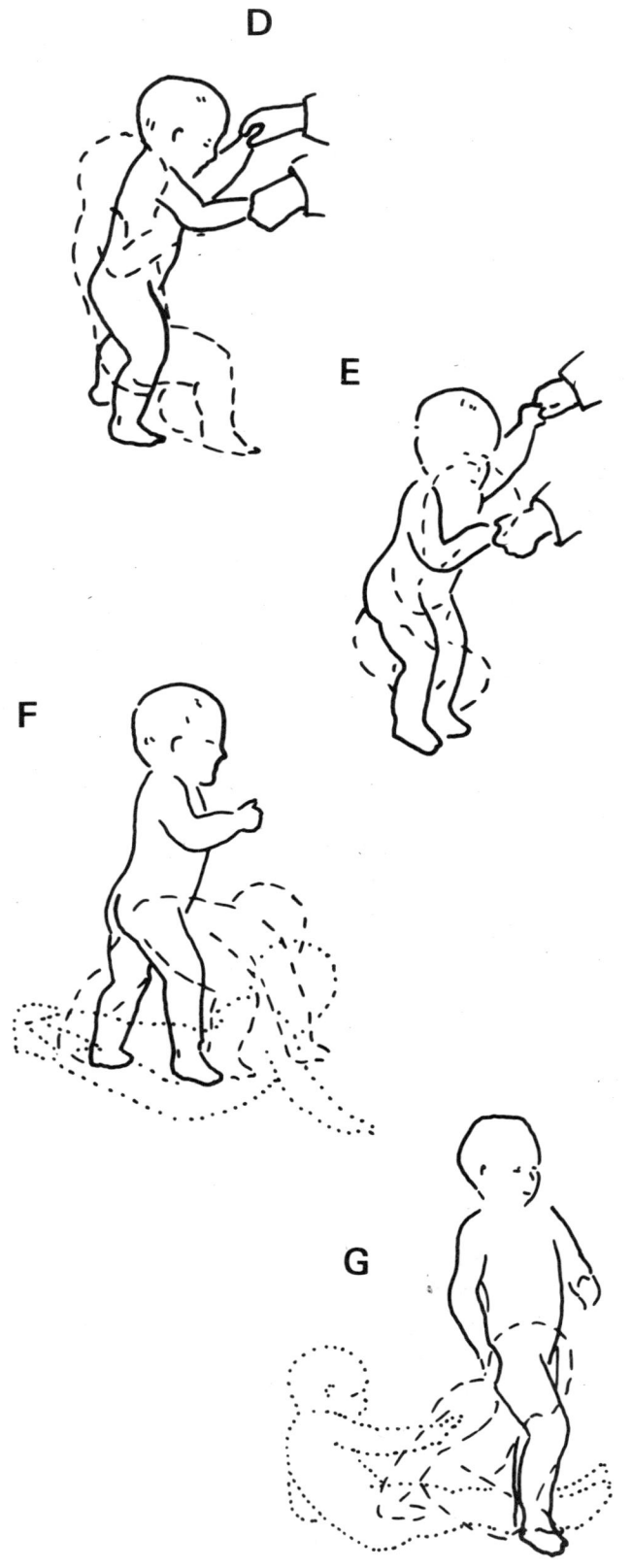

D

E

F

G

5. Almost as soon as you take the baby's hands she places her feet on the surface, brings shoulders forward and then pushes her body upward so that she straightens her legs. By this time the baby has probably begun to pull herself up by the bars of the crib (E).
   Date_____ Yes_____ No_____

6. The baby can pull himself up by the side of the crib, but can't let himself down.
   Date_____ Yes_____ No_____

7. The baby can pull herself up by the side of the crib, and also carefully let herself down (F).
   Date_____ Yes_____ No_____

8. The infant can get from a reclining to a standing position without assistance. In doing this he first rolls over from back to stomach.
   Date_____ Yes_____ No_____

9. The baby no longer rolls over onto the stomach before getting up. She places her feet and one hand on the floor, then pushes upward in a well co-ordinated movement (G).
   Date_____ Yes_____ No_____

RECORD 99

Questionnaire for Only Children
(TO BE FILLED OUT BY SIXTEEN- TO TWENTY-FOUR-YEAR-OLD CHILDREN)
(A Researcher's Record)

EDITOR'S NOTE Circle T or F unless otherwise indicated. Also, feel free to add words to the T/F statements, write in margins, or otherwise personalize these pages. Questionnaires will be individually read, not machine-scored. Xerox the filled-out record, forward to the Princeton Center for Infancy, and we will forward it to the researcher.

T F   1. I am very glad I am an only child.
T F   2. I am generally glad I am an only child.
T F   3. I often regret being an only child.
T F   4. I sometimes regret being an only child.
T F   5. I have no particular positive or negative feelings about my "onliness."
T F   6. I have had no particular *awareness* of my "onliness."
       7. Compared to others I know, I feel I am (Write in "more," "less" or "equally"):

   _____ successful   _____ relaxed about life in general
   _____ co-operative   _____ satisfied with self
   _____ spoiled   _____ satisfied with career achievement
   _____ lonely   _____ satisfied with social adjustment
   _____ intelligent   _____ satisfied with sexual adjustment
   _____ accomplished   _____ satisfied with total adjustment

T F   8. I always wanted a sister/brother. (Circle one *true*.)
T F   9. I only recall wanting a sister or brother
T F   in preschool years
T F   in elementary school
T F   in high school
T F   college or after high school
T F   as an adult
T F   10. I never wanted a brother or sister.
T F   11. I knew other only children when I was growing up.
T F   12. I had a "fantasy" brother or sister or friend as a child.
T F   13. I sometimes pretended a friend was my brother or sister.
T F   14. I had many friends as a child.
T F   15. I have many friends now.
T F   16. I prefer a few close friends to a large number of casual ones.
T F   17. I have discussed with my parents their reasons for having only me.
       18. If "True," please explain their reasons briefly.

   _____
   _____

RECORD 99 (CONTINUED)

19. If "False," why was this not discussed and what do you believe their reasons were?
_____
_____

20. Do you feel your parents benefited from having only you? If so, how? _____
_____
_____

21. What are advantages you feel *you* enjoyed as an only child? (If none, write "None.") _____
_____
_____

21. As an adult? _____
_____
_____

22. List any disadvantages you feel you had or have. (If none, write "None.") _____
_____
_____

23. What *negative remarks*, if any, have you been subject to about your "onliness"? Please list, and explain circumstances briefly. _____
_____
_____

24. What are your responses to the above negative remarks? _____
_____
_____

25. My own preferred number of children to have would be _____ and the number of children I have now is _____.
26. I believe prejudice against the only child is (Circle one): slight–moderate–severe.

T F 27. If there were an association for only children, and families with a single child who face pressure to have another child, I would be interested.
T F 28. In having or thinking about having a child or children, I would be willing to adopt.
29. My parents are (Circle one): married–divorced–separated–separated by death.
30. My parents' ages when they had me were: Mother _____ father _____
T F 31. I live with my parents, or one of them.
32. If you won honors in school (e.g. prom queen, honor society) please list them.
_____
_____
_____

RECORD 99 (CONTINUED)

33. If you have won recognition in your work, please list awards, honors, other types of recognition. _____
_____
_____

34. I am (Circle one): single—married—separated—divorced—involved in a stable but nonmarital relationship.

T F 35. I am content with above status.
T F 36. If married, my spouse's birth order is (Circle one): only—eldest—middle—youngest.
      37. I support the following ideas:
T F   women's liberation (major goals)
T F   reform of campaign financing
T F   guaranteed annual income
T F   gun control
T F   increased benefits for the aged
T F   zero population growth
T F   strict environmental controls

38. My sex is _____ and my age is _____ .

39. Topics which this questionnaire failed to mention but which are relevant to the only child include:

_____
_____
_____
_____
_____
_____
_____
_____
_____
_____

RECORD 100   Recorder _____

Questionnaire for Parents of Only Children
(A Researcher's Record)

Circle T or F unless otherwise indicated. However, feel free to add words to the T/F statements, write in margins, or otherwise personalize this questionnaire. Responses *will* be individually read. Xerox the filled-out record, forward to the Princeton Center for Infancy, and we will forward it to the researcher. (Xerox for other parent.)

T F   1. My having an only child was a deliberate decision.
T F   2. I am very glad I have just one child.
T F   3. I am generally glad I have just one child.
T F   4. I often regret having just one child.
T F   5. I sometimes regret having just one child.
        6. Compared to other children of my child's peer group, I feel my child is (Write in "more," "less," "equally"):

   _____ co-operative   _____ lonely
   _____ successful in school   _____ intelligent
   _____ popular   _____ creative and imaginative
   _____ spoiled   _____ happy

   A specific incident in which I have observed my child being (more, less, equally) *co-operative* in comparison to other children is (Please describe—perhaps a play situation): _____
   _____
   _____

        7. My own birth-order situation is _____ (only, eldest, middle, youngest) from a family of _____ children.
        8. My spouse is _____ (only, eldest, etc.) from a family of _____ children.
T F   9. I have been criticized for having just one child.
        10. My only child is a boy, girl (circle one), age _____ .
T F   11. I believe my only child has been made aware of her "onliness."
        12. I believe my child is happy to be an only child _____
            (always, generally, sometimes, never, other comment).
        12a. My child has expressed a wish for a brother or sister _____
            (often, sometimes, never).
T F   13. If my child expresses a wish for a sibling, I believe this is partly due to attitudes of peers and their families. _____
            _____
            _____

14. Why, and *when*, did you decide to have only one child? (Please explain in as much detail as you wish.) _____
_____
_____

15. Have you definitely decided to have only one child?
16. If "No," on what factors will your decision rest? (economic, social criticism, others) _____
17. What advantages do *you* feel you have had, have now, and will have in the future as a result of having only one child? _____
_____
_____

18. What advantages do you feel your child has had and will have? _____
_____
_____

19. Please comment on any disadvantages you see for you or your child. _____
_____

20. I believe social prejudice against one-child families to be (Circle one): negligible—slight—moderate—serious—so severe as to jeopardize many individuals' decision to have only one child.
21. What criticisms have you received as the parent of an only child? (Please describe as many as you recall, and state circumstances briefly.) _____
_____
_____

22. What are your responses to the above criticisms? _____
_____
_____

23. Have you ever found yourself seeking out articles or books which would help justify your decision? _____
_____
_____
_____

24. Do you feel that sufficient articles or books exist on the subject?
25. If you knew of a rap group in your town or city for parents of only children, would you attend?
26. If there were an association for parents of one child, would you be interested?
_____

RECORD 100 (CONTINUED)

27. I support the following ideas:
- T F women's liberation
- T F reform of campaign financing
- T F guaranteed annual income
- T F gun control
- T F zero population growth
- T F increased benefits for aged
- T F strict environmental controls

28. Do you feel your relationship with your spouse would improve, worsen, or remain the same if you had another child? (Circle one)

29. Do you feel your relationship with your child would improve, worsen, or remain the same if you had another child? (Circle one)

30. How do you feel other goals in your life (other than parenthood) would be affected by another increase in your family size? _____

31. My sex is _____. My age is _____. My marital status is (Circle one): single—married—separated—divorced—stable but nonmarital relationship.

32. Topics which I wish this questionnaire had brought up, but which it failed to bring up, include: _____

- T F 33. (If living separately) I visit my parent(s) often.
- T F 34. My parent(s) complain that I am inattentive.
- T F 35. I feel my parent(s) are too dependent on me financially.
- T F 36. I feel my parent(s) are too dependent on me emotionally.
- T F 37. I fear my parent(s)' emotional dependence on me in later years.
- T F 38. I fear my parent(s)' financial dependence on me in later years.
- 39. My job is (Circle one): professional—secretarial—clerical—mechanical—other.
- 40. My work is in the field of (Circle one): transportation—education—arts—sciences—government—public service—factory—social reform—other.
- T F 41. My devotion to my work is such that recreation is minimal.
- T F 42. My co-workers are among my best friends.
- 43. Briefly describe your social or recreational life, including: favorite activities, number of evenings out in a typical week, whether you prefer large or small gatherings, etc. _____

44. If you have supported with time or money a community theater, church group, museum, improvement association, political organization, etc., please list: _____

45. My childhood hobbies included: _____

Glossary

Alerting child shows sign of attention by interrupting his or her activity (raising the head, for example).

Amniocentesis a technique by which a hollow needle is used to draw a sampling of the amniotic fluid that surrounds the fetus. Tests can tell sex, genetic malformations, age of fetus, etc.

Attends concentrates, shows active interest, follows, responds to various stimuli.

Babbles makes spontaneous, nonarticulated sounds (murmurs, coos, gurgles). Baby practices inflection and intonation as a forerunner of speech.

Biological parent the natural parent (as distinguished from an adoptive parent).

Cognition a child's style or approach to learning.

Cortex the outer layer of gray matter covering the brain (cerebrum and cerebellum). As it matures, it gains increasing control over body actions and sensory feelings.

Cough game takes place when the parent initiates a dry cough and the baby responds as part of an interaction process that will be played over and over again.

"Critical period" there is an approximate age range during which parents may expect readiness for new learnings to occur. The critical period covers the time span most propitious to the cultivation of specific skills by means of intervention and encouragement.

Derivative citizenship a means of securing U.S. citizenship by virtue of the fact that the foreign-born parents became citizens before their child was 21, thus automatically giving him or her full citizenship rights.

Down's Syndrome also known as Mongolism, occurs in 3 births out of 1,000. It is a common cause of mental retardation due to genetic abnormality of the chromosomes. (Facial and head features also are distorted.)

Fetal describes the condition of the infant in the womb during the pregnancy period.

Fetal position the position of the fetus in the birth canal of the mother.

Fetalogy this new field in obstetrics is the study of human development from microscopic cells to fully formed infant floating in a liquid prenatal environment.

Genetic counseling the science of predicting the possibility of birth defects by means of the study of altered or misplaced chromosomes, faulty genes, and family health histories. Genetic counseling can alert parents to any possibility of inherited birth defects in *advance* of a pregnancy.

H, A, L abbreviations for *High, Average, Low*.

Kinesthetic sensory stimuli; experiences with handling, grasping, pulling, feeling, etc.

Labeling verbally labeling everything the baby sees and does—for instance, the word "book" when the child touches or turns the pages of a book, "down" when child falls, "ball" when a ball is handled, etc. It promotes language acquisition.

Nasopalpebral reflex tapping the bridge of the nose of an infant causes automatic blinking of both eyes.

"Onset" or "entry" date the time period in which the skill under study makes its first appearance in the infant. Onset is not to be confused with mastery; it takes several months before a child masters an activity. Progress often is slow and uneven, even regressive on occasion. Record "onset" in months and weeks (6 mos. 2 wks), weeks and days (2 wks. 3 days), whichever is most appropriate.

Peripheral vision vision on the outer boundaries of the eyes.

Preverbal communication indicates the interaction that precedes words, sentences, and language. It takes the forms of infant gestures, head turning, facial expressions, etc. which the responsive parent "reads."

Pupillary action: the reaction of the pupils of the eyes to following or tracking an object in an infant's field of vision.

Rh factor this refers to the compatibility or incompatibility of the blood of the pregnant woman and her fetus.

Rhythmicity implies that a child has a "built-in regulatory system"; for instance, she or he will awaken at the same time every day, have a predictable fussy time, etc.

Rooming-in the type of hospital accommodations whereby the newborn baby is brought to the mother in the morning after breakfast and remains with her until bedtime. It allows both parents to get to know their infant and to practice routines from *day one*.

Rooting reflex an involuntary (automatic) movement that appears at birth and occurs only when the infant is awake. For example, if you stimulate the cheek by finger pressure, the baby's head will turn toward the finger and the baby will open his or her mouth (often this is utilized by mothers to help the baby feed at the breast).

Siblings brothers or sisters of a child.

Socialization the process of give and take for establishing interpersonal relations between parents and child, child and siblings, and child and strangers or others.

Spontaneous reflexes these are patterned movements that the newborn uses instinctively in response to stimuli from the environment. Some are fully developed at birth; others will become better organized in time; and still others are transient reflexes that will undergo gradual extinction because they are no longer needed for survival.

Toxemia symptoms during the latter part of pregnancy that take the forms of puffiness of face, eyes, or fingers, blurring of vision, etc.

Tracking the baby's following with eyes and head an object that is in the path of his or her vision.

Vocalization early attempts by the baby (from the third through the eighth months) to imitate the sounds of voices he or she hears in the environment.